MW01094197

The Gluten Free Mediterranean Diet Cookbook

150 Delicious and Healthy Recipes

Chef Judi Mehrens

© Copyright 2013 Chef Judi Mehrens & Smiling Partners Publishing

All rights reserved. No part of this book may be reproduced by any means whatsoever without the written permission from the author, except brief portions quoted for purpose of review.

Any and all information contained herein is not intended to take the place of medical advice from a healthcare professional. This information is for educational and informational purposes only. Readers should always consult with a physician before taking any actions of any kind relating to their health. The author nor publisher will in no way be held responsible for any reader who fails to do so. Any action taken based on these contents is at the sole discretion and liability of the reader.

All information in this book has been carefully researched and checked for factual accuracy. However, the author and publisher make no warranty, express or implied, that the information contained herein is appropriate for every individual, situation, or purpose, and assumes no responsibility for errors or omissions. The reader assumes the risk and full responsibility for all actions, and the author will not be held responsible for any loss or damage, whether consequential, incidental, special or otherwise that may result from the information presented in this publication.

Table of Contents

Opening Notes

Thank you for buying this book. I've tried to provide gluten-free alternatives that are healthy and tasty. I hope you'll find that I've succeeded.

This is a compilation of three volumes of my previously published Gluten Free Mediterranean Cookbooks. I haven't changed much here from those three recipe books, other than a few typos here and there (how did those get through??).

However, I did find some things that weren't as clear as I'd hoped, or that I thought could use further explanation. So here goes:

1. I cannot stress enough the importance of reading – studying – the labels of every bit of prepared food that you shop for. Even things you believe can't possibly contain gluten can surprise you. I discovered a while ago that a favorite prepared chicken stock contains wheat gluten. It's big and bold on the label; I just hadn't bothered looking. Who would think chicken stock, of all things, would contain wheat gluten. It certainly wasn't an ingredient of the stock I was taught to make in culinary school.

Again, the important thing is vigilance.

2. Rather than a strict "eat only this and lose weight" diet, this is a lifestyle diet. That's why there are no calorie counts. If you follow the basics of this style of eating – plenty of fresh vegetables, lean protein (fish and poultry), and eat it in moderation, combined with regular exercise of some sort, you'll be healthier and very likely lose weight.

3. While fresh ingredients are an important part of the Mediterranean diet, it's perfectly fine to use canned when you need to. Sometimes the tomatoes in the market aren't worth buying; in that case, it's okay to use canned. If you forgot to soak the beans overnight, certainly use the canned. As with all your ingredients, use the best you can find and can afford.

4. A Mediterranean diet relies heavily on fish, and there are probably species listed that are unfamiliar or unavailable to you. Or these varieties might be very expensive where you live. Just keep in mind that substitution is always an option. Same goes if you just don't like a particular fish.

Starting this diet, then, would provide a very good time for you to get to know your local purveyor of seafood, or at least the manager of your local store's seafood counter. I am lucky enough to live in the Pacific Northwest, where we have abundant fish available and lots of fish markets. If you are limited in options, it makes it more important to get to know whoever it is providing your fish.

Another note about fish: if you're buying a whole fish, look at its eyes. They should be clear and not cloudy to guarantee freshness. Also don't be afraid to ask to smell the fish. There should be a slightly briny odor. If it smells strongly "fishy," you might want to find another market.

There is nothing wrong with buying frozen fish, either. Much of the fish you'll find at the fish counter has been previously frozen anyway. Commercial fishers more often than not flash freeze their catch before they ever get to shore.

5. Cooking fish can seem tricky, but it's really not. James

Beard, one of our great Northwest chefs and cookbook writers, suggested cooking fish for 10 minutes per inch of thickness. I've found this to be a very good, easily remembered guideline, no matter the cooking method.

6. There are a number of recipes here that list wine or other spirits as an ingredient. Generally, any of the alcohol is cooked out of the dish before it every reaches the table. However, if you'd just prefer not to include it, substituting chicken or vegetable broth is perfectly fine. There will be a little taste variation, but the end result will still be tasty.

7. You will see that there are some recipes for veal included here. I know there are some folks who object to veal. And others, like me, who find veal difficult to find, very expensive, and without much taste when raised commercially. Whatever the reason, a boneless, skinless chicken breast is an acceptable substitute. Just be sure to pound the breast thin, breaking down the shoulder and allowing the meat to cook evenly. Cook the chicken long enough to be sure it's done through, generally 3 or 4 minutes per side.

On that note, an easy way to process the chicken is to put it into a plastic storage bag. Lay it flat inside the bag, and then you can pound it gently with your kitchen mallet. I say gently because if you go at the meat too vigorously, you'll end up with splattered pieces. You're looking for a flat even thickness. The bag allows you to see what you're doing without making a mess on your counter.

8. There are a few recipes that call for sectioned oranges in the ingredients. This means the orange has none of the pith, the white part, attached, and that the sections are free of

membrane. This is easier than it might sound:

Cut off the top and bottom of the orange. Now set the orange on a flat end, and using your sharp knife, start cutting off the rind and pith in pieces, curving around to the bottom. You'll lose some of the orange itself, just try to cut as close as you can while making sure none of the pith remains attached. Now, holding the orange over a bowl to catch the juices, slice next to the membranes on each side to release the sections. It might take a few tries, but by the time you're done with one orange, you'll have this technique down.

9. Fresh basil is an important ingredient in many of these recipes, sometimes chopped finely and sometimes in strips, or chiffonade. An easy way to cut these strips is to trim the stem from the leaf, and then to roll up the leaf or leaves into a cylinder. Simply then cut the cylinder crosswise into small pieces. Unroll and you have nice strips of basil.

10. I haven't included any recipes for pasta, primarily because at the time of writing these books I hadn't found a good gluten-free option. That all changed a few months ago when my husband and I were out with friends for meal at a local high-end Italian restaurant. One of our party has a gluten intolerance and noticed a gluten-free option for pasta. He tried it, shared it, and we were all blown away. We asked the waiter what it was, and he brought the package out to us.

The pasta was made by Tinkyada, a company I later found out makes an entire line of just about any style of pasta you might want. It's a rice pasta, and they offer both white and brown rice versions. I haven't tried the brown rice variety, but the white is indistinguishable from wheat pasta. In fact, we had a family gathering where I fixed a big pot of spaghetti using Tinkyada, and not a single person could tell it was gluten free.

If you crave pasta and you've had it up to here with the mushy, gooey, bad tasting stuff offered as gluten free, try Tinkyada. There are several stores in our area that carry some of the products, so check out your local supermarkets. If you can't find it, check online. Amazon.com is just one of the places where you can order it online.

11. Another gluten free product I've found that I highly recommend is Domata Living Flour. You can use it in the same proportion as regular flour in most of your recipes, with only the smallest difference in texture. Actually in most things, you'd have to have side by side comparison with a wheat flour preparation to even notice. And the brownie recipe they have online (their web site can be found at http://domataglutenfree.com/) makes the best brownies I've ever had, wheat or not.

The flour is not cheap, but I have no reservation in saying it's well worth the money. You can buy it from their website and on amazon.com, where you can read the reviews.

So now on to the recipes.

I've changed the organization of the recipes, putting them into categories, so that, hopefully, it will be easier for you to find just what you're looking for.

Happy cooking!

Original Introduction

This book came about because of my ongoing interest in all

things gluten free and my newfound interest in the Mediterranean diet.

My sister and niece both have celiac sprue disease, which means their systems cannot process food that has gluten in it. Ingesting gluten can have all kinds of bad effects on the health of anyone who has the disease.

Whether you have this disease or you have just decided to eliminate gluten from your diet, one of the most important things you need to learn to do is to read the labels on the food you're looking to buy.

Being gluten free isn't just about taking bread and pasta out of your diet. You'll be amazed at how many foods have gluten in them. You'll also start to notice just how much salt and sugar are in processed foods.

This diet is about avoiding those processed foods, but if you must use them, be sure that you know what you're buying.

While I don't have a gluten intolerance, I do have an ongoing battle with my weight. I've been on just about every diet out there, and I'm constantly looking at how I can eat in a more healthy way while maintaining some sort of weight control, but I'm done with eating boring tasteless food.

The Mediterranean diet has recently caught my attention for a couple of reasons: it is healthy and it has food that tastes good. There are a lot of studies out there showing how people who eat in the Mediterranean style are healthier and live longer!

Eating Mediterranean means eating fresh and healthy, and in many cases, with quick and easy recipes. It means that you'll be using very little butter, instead using healthy olive oil. As with any good recipe, you'll want to find the freshest and best quality ingredients that you can afford.

Beef is an occasional ingredient; fish and poultry are more common, with smaller portions, 3 to 4 ounces or so. You'll be eating more vegetables, but prepared in a way that might surprise you with their good taste.

Fruit is your delicious dessert treat, again prepared in more interesting ways, although plain fresh fruit is a good ending to any meal. Or a good snack.

Nuts, particularly almonds, are also an excellent snack. The nut oils are especially healthy.

Another healthy aspect of this way eating is that Mediterranean meals are leisurely affairs. Taking time to sit at the table for a real sit-down meal is something not too many modern families - or even individuals - do. An important part of any diet, whether to lose weight or just to be more healthy, is to take time to actually sit at a table, without distraction, slowly enjoying the meal.

Herbs are an important addition for flavor. Again, fresh are best, but dried herbs are an okay substitution, adding to the taste of your food and eliminating the need for a lot of salt.

If you enjoy wine, have a glass with dinner. It seems that just about every day we see a new study showing the health benefits of wine in moderation, lately especially for women.

These recipes should be viewed as a reference point, perhaps new ideas in cooking techniques. You might want to try them as written, to get a sense of the idea, but then feel free to substitute the ingredients that you can find or that taste better to you. The beauty of the Mediterranean way of cooking and eating is that it primarily relies on what is fresh and available.

Let your inner chef find its path!

I. Appetizers, Salads, and Sauces

Apple And Onion Jam

Here's an excellent topping for chicken or pork.

1 tablespoon extra virgin olive oil
3 cups diced onions
1 cup finely diced apple
1/2 teaspoon salt
2 tablespoons sugar
1 tablespoon apple cider vinegar
1 tablespoon water

Heat olive oil over medium low heat. Add onions, apple, and salt. Cook for 15 minutes, occasionally stirring. Add the sugar, vinegar, and water, and continue cooking for another 20 to 25 minutes, until you have the consistency of a thick jam.

Baby Beet Salad

Truly a salad for beet lovers. Baby beets have a sweeter and fresher taste than their big brothers.

16 baby beets, stems trimmed
1 cup mixed baby greens
extra virgin olive oil
salt and pepper

Preheat oven to 375 degrees F.

Wrap the beets individually in foil and roast in the middle of the oven until fork tender, 30 to 40 minutes. Remove from the oven and let them rest in the foil for 15 minutes. Carefully open the foil, taking care of the steam.

Cut off the stems and peel. Cut them in halves or quarters and arrange over the greens. Drizzle the olive oil over and season with salt and pepper. Best served at room temperature.

Bean and Tuna Salad

This is a great throw-it-together meal. You can use canned beans or freshly cooked, any variety that you prefer, and you can change up the herbs for a different taste.

1 thinly sliced red onion
4 tablespoons red wine vinegar
2 cups cooked white beans
1 - 6.5 ounce can water packed tuna, drained
2 tomatoes, diced
1 garlic clove, minced
juice of 1 lemon
4 tablespoons chopped fresh basil
1 teaspoon chopped fresh sage
2 tablespoons olive oil
1 tablespoon capers, rinsed
salt and pepper to taste

Put the onions in a container, add 3 tablespoons of the vinegar, and cover with water. Let them soak for 30 minutes, then drain.

Toss the remaining tablespoon of vinegar with the onions and the rest of the ingredients. Garnish with tomato wedges and serve on a bed of lettuce.

Beet and Potato Salad

Besides having a great taste, this is a very pretty dish. Add to it by serving a scoop onto a lettuce leaf or cup.

2 large beets, peeled, steamed until tender
2 large potatoes, scrubbed, steamed until tender
2 tablespoons white wine vinegar
2 tablespoons fresh lemon juice
1 clove minced garlic
2 teaspoons caraway seeds, slightly crushed
salt and pepper to taste
1 tablespoon olive oil
2 tablespoons fresh parsley, chopped

Let beets and potatoes cool, then slice thinly. Mix the remaining ingredients, taste for seasoning, then gently toss with the beets and potatoes. Refrigerate before serving.

Broiled Mushrooms

A simple and delicious preparation, mushroom lovers will appreciate this appetizer.

1 pound large mushrooms, cleaned and stems removed
1 tablespoon olive oil
3 cloves garlic, sliced thinly
1/2 teaspoon dried rosemary, crumbled
1/4 teaspoon dried thyme
salt and pepper to taste

Heat the broiler. Lightly oil a baking sheet.

Put the mushrooms on the baking sheet, stem side up. Drizzle the olive oil over them, then sprinkle on the garlic, herbs, and salt and pepper. Broil for 15 minutes, brushing occasionally with any juices in the pan, turning the mushrooms over after 10 minutes.

Caponata

Even if you think you don't like eggplant, you might find your mind changes when you taste this delicious dish. Try it with vegetable chips for dipping or as a tasty sauce for grilled chicken or fish.

2 medium eggplants, peeled and diced into 1 inch cubes
4 ripe tomatoes
salt
2 large red peppers, seeded and cut into 1 inch pieces
2 medium zucchini, scrubbed and sliced 1/4 inch thick
2 medium onions, thinly sliced
4 cloves garlic, chopped
2 heaping tablespoons capers, rinsed
1 bay leaf
1/2 teaspoon fresh thyme
salt and black pepper
1/4 cup white wine or cider vinegar
1 1/2 teaspoons sugar
1 tablespoon olive oil
chopped parsley

Put the eggplant in a colander in the sink and generously sprinkle with salt. Let sit for an hour. Rinse and pat dry.

Heat the tomatoes in a pan over low heat for about 15 minutes. Season with a pinch of salt, then mash them with the back of a spoon.

Heat the oven to 350 degrees F. Generously oil a roasting pan big enough for all the vegetables.

Combine the vegetables, garlic, capers, bay leaf, thyme and salt and pepper in the pan.

Combine the vinegar and sugar and heat just until the sugar melts. Add it and the olive oil to the vegetables and toss everything to mix it all up well. Cover the baking pan tightly with foil and bake for 1 1/2 to 2 hours, turning the vegetables several times during the baking, until the vegetables are cooked through.

Remove the pan from the oven and allow the vegetables to cool. Then cover and refrigerate overnight. Serve at room temperature.

Cherry Tomato Salad

If you can find varieties of tomatoes of different colors, this looks like a work of art! You can make this salad with fresh tomato wedges, too.

3 pints small tomatoes, assorted with whatever is available, cut in half
1 bunch fresh basil, cut into fine strips
3 minced shallots
1/4 cup balsamic vinegar
2 tablespoons red wine vinegar
1 tablespoon minced garlic
salt and pepper
3/4 cup olive oil

Put the tomatoes into a large bowl and add the basil strips.

In a separate bowl, mix together the shallots, vinegars, garlic, and salt and pepper. Set aside for 10 to 15 minutes for the flavors to combine.

Whisk the oil into the vinegar mix, a little at a time. Toss gently with the tomatoes and basil.

Correct the seasoning, if necessary.

Chickpea Salad With Yogurt Dressing

The scallion, radish, and green pepper add appealing color to the salad. The yogurt dressing brings everything together for great taste. Pretty when served in lettuce cups, as well.

3 - 19 ounce cans chick peas, drained and rinsed
4 scallions, chopped
4 radishes, sliced
1 green pepper, seeded and chopped
1/2 cup chopped fresh parsley
2 tablespoons grated Parmesan cheese

Yogurt Vinaigrette

juice of 1 lemon
3 tablespoons white wine or champagne vinegar
1 garlic clove, minced
2 teaspoons Dijon mustard
3/4 cup plain low fat yogurt

Heat the chick peas, then toss with the vegetables and cheese.

Mix the vinaigrette ingredients well, then toss with the chick pea mixture. Serve at room temperature or warmed a bit.

Cucumber and Yogurt Sauce

This is a sauce that adds greatly to raw vegetables as well as grilled meat and fish. It's the tzatziki sauce used on gyros sandwiches. If you prefer, add more garlic!

1 tablespoon olive oil
1 teaspoon wine vinegar
1 garlic clove, minced
8 ounces plain low fat yogurt
1 4 inch cucumber, peeled, grated, and drained

1 tablespoon finely chopped fresh mint

Whisk the olive oil and vinegar together, add the garlic, then the yogurt, and mix well. Fold in the grated cucumber and mint. Cover and refrigerate for a couple of hours before serving, so the flavors blend.

Curry Quinoa Salad With Raisins

This salad would traditionally be made with couscous, but I've adapted it to use quinoa, a completely gluten free alternative. The raisins are a nice counter to the curry in this salad, as is the orange zest. The salad can be served chilled or at room temperature.

Quinoa is becoming more available in the health food sections of markets, or it can readily be found online.

2 tablespoons extra virgin olive oil, separated
1 cup quinoa
2 cups warm water
1/3 cup golden raisins
1/2 teaspoon curry power
1 clove finely minced garlic
1/2 cup bell pepper, cored and finely chopped
1/2 cup finely diced celery
4 minced scallions
1 teaspoon orange zest
1/2 teaspoon salt
1/8 teaspoon black pepper
1/4 cup toasted pin nuts

Heat 1 tablespoon olive oil over medium heat. Add the quinoa and allow to toast about 3 minutes, stirring occasionally. Add the warm water, raisins, and curry powder. Mix well, bring to a boil, reduce to a simmer, and cover the pot. Cook 15 minutes or until the liquid is all absorbed. Put into a bowl to cool.

To the cooled couscous add the rest of the ingredients, including the reserved 1 tablespoon olive oi. Mix well and check the seasonings. Refrigerate at least 30 minutes to blend the flavors.

Eggplant Salad

This is another salad you'll want to serve in a lettuce cup or on top of a colorful lettuce assortment. It tastes amazing with the garlic and lemon for flavoring.

2 pounds eggplant, cut in half
3 garlic cloves, mashed
juice of 2 lemons
salt and pepper to taste
1 tablespoon olive oil

Heat the broiler. Oil a baking pan.

Put the cut side of the eggplant on the baking pan, then broil until the skin is wrinkled and charred and the eggplant is soft. Allow to cool.

Scoop the eggplant pulp from the skin and put into a blender. Puree, then add the rest of the ingredients.

Fava Bean Salad

The combination of beans and the bright flavors presented here are sure to please. This salad can be served well chilled or brought back to room temperature.

1 1/4 cups dried white fava beans
3 sage leaves
Salt
2 cloves minced garlic

1 finely chopped onion
1 finely chopped celery stalk
3 tablespoons lemon juice
1/2 teaspoon dried oregano
3 tablespoons olive oil
4 tablespoons white wine vinegar
salt and pepper

Soak the beans in water overnight. Drain, rinse, and put into a pot with 4 cups water, and bring to a boil. Add the sage and salt to taste, cover the pot, and let simmer for about an hour, until the beans are soft but not mushy.

Remove from the heat and drain. Let the beans cool a bit, then add the rest of the ingredients, mixing gently. Chill before serving.

Fennel Salad

Fennel is one of my favorite things, both cooked and raw. The flavor combination of this salad is most pleasing.

1 clove garlic, cut in half lengthwise
1 large fennel bulb, trimmed and thinly sliced
1/2 cucumber, thinly sliced
1 tablespoon chives, minced
8 radishes, thinly sliced
2 tablespoons olive oil
2 tablespoons lemon juice
salt and pepper

Use the cut garlic side to rub the inside of your salad bowl. Add the fennel, cucumber, chives, and radishes. Separately whisk the olive oil, lemon juice, and salt and pepper. Drizzle over the salad, and then mix gently.

Fresh Mozzarella With Tomato and Basil

If you can find it, bocconcini, a mozarella-like cheese made from water buffalo milk, is the preferred ingredient. It can often be found at specialty Italian markets. If you can't find it, a good quality fresh mozzarella makes a fine dish.

Add a drizzle of balsamic vinegar for a different taste.

2 fresh mozzarella balls, about 4 ounces
2 medium ripe tomatoes
15 large basil leaves, separated
2 teaspoons extra virgin olive oil
salt and freshly ground black pepper to taste

Slice the mozzarella into a total of 8 slices. Core and slice the tomatoes into a total of 8 slices.

Keep 8 basil leaves whole, then shred the rest.

Layer one tomato slice, 1 mozzarella slice, and 1 basil leaf, making 4 stacks on two plates. Drizzle with olive oil, and garnish with the shredded basil.

Serves 2.

Fresh Tomato Sauce

Just plain delicious! Gently heat and use as a topping to quickly broiled or sauteed meat or seafood.

2 pounds ripe red tomatoes, peeled, seeded, and chopped
3 garlic cloves, minced
4 tablespoons chopped fresh basil
2 tablespoons balsamic vinegar
salt and pepper
2 small hot chili peppers, chopped (Optional)

10

Combine all the ingredients, mixing gently. Refrigerate or keep at room temperature for an hour or two for the flavors to combine.

Grated Carrot and Yogurt Salad

Another tasty way to health. The sweetness of the carrots is complemented nicely by the yogurt.

6 medium carrots
2 minced garlic cloves
1 teaspoon salt
1/4 cup plain yogurt
2 teaspoons olive oil
2 teaspoons lemon juice

Bring a pot of water to boil and add the carrots. Cook for 5 minutes, then take the carrots out of the pot and plunge them into an ice bath. When they're cool enough to handle, grate them coarsely.

In a separate bowl and using the back of a spoon, crush the garlic and salt together. Add the rest of the ingredients, and check for seasoning, adding more salt or lemon juice as desired.

Greek Peasant Salad

A bit of chopping and mixing and you have a delicious salad for a starter or to stand on its own. Buy the best, most flavorful olive oil you can find.

3/4 pound tomatoes, trimmed, cut into wedges
1 red onion, quartered, then thinly sliced
1/2 green pepper, seeds removed and sliced thinly
small cucumber, thinly sliced
8 pitted black olives

1/4 pound feta cheese, crumbled
3 tablespoons olive oil
salt and pepper
1/4 teaspoon dried oregano

Put the tomatoes, onion, pepper, cucumber, olives, and 2 tablespoons olive oil in a bowl and combine gently, making sure the oil is distributed evenly. Season with salt and pepper. Add the feta and drizzle the remaining tablespoon of oil over. Sprinkle with the oregano and serve.

Green Bean and Cannellini Salad

A tasty way to serve green beans, the cold water bath stops the cooking and leaves them crunchy and fresh. This also serves as a wonderful side dish or a filling main course.

1 pound sliced young green beans, cut into 1 inch pieces
salt
1/2 onion, thinly sliced
1 - 15 ounce cannellini beans, drained and rinsed
3 tablespoons olive oil
2 tablespoons sherry vinegar
black pepper

Add string beans to 2 quarts boiling, salted water, and boil for 5 minutes. Drain the beans and put them into an ice water bath, stopping them from cooking any more. Drain well and dry.

Mix the beans, onion, and cannellini beans gently. In a separate bowl whisk the olive oil, vinegar, and pepper until they're well mixed. Add the dressing to the beans and stir to combine. Best served at toom temperature.

Green Olive and Lentil Salad

I love green olives, and this dish lets me have them in a healthy way. Their tartness, the sweetness of the pepper, and the zip of the lemon juice and zest combine in a very tasty and attractive way.

1/2 pound lentils, picked over, rinsed, and drained
1 small onion, halved
1 clove garlic
1 bay leaf
1 cup green olives, pitted and chopped
1 sweet pepper, sliced
1/3 cup olive oil
3 tablespoons lemon juice
salt and pepper
zest of 1/2 lemon, grated
1/4 cup chopped parsley

Combine the lentils with 3 cups water, the onion, garlic, and bay leaf. Bring to a boil, then turn down the heat, cover the pan, and simmer for 30 minutes, until the lentils are tender. Drain the lentils, picking out and discarding the onion, garlic, and bay leaf.

Let the lentils cool a bit, then toss with the olives, pepper, olive oil, lemon juice, and seasonings. Garnish with the zest and parsley.

Hummus

Serve this delicious and healthy dip with a plate of crunchy vegetables.

Tahini is a sesame paste that should be found in your grocer's international foods section. Or you can make it yourself by toasting 5 cups sesame seeds in a 350 degree oven for 5 to 10 minutes, tossing them frequently. Cool the seeds and put them into a food processor. Add 1 1/2 cups of the lightest tasting olive oil you can find. Blend for a couple of minutes until you have a thick but pourable paste. Add more oil if needed for consistency. Keep it sealed in the refrigerator for up to 3 weeks.

2 cloves garlic, peeled
2 - 15 ounce cans of garbanzo beans, drained, saving the liquid
2 tablespoons lemon juice
2 tablespoons extra virgin olive oil
2 tablespoons tahini
4 teaspoons ground coriander
2 teaspoons cumin
1/2 tablespoon sale
1/8 teaspoon freshly ground black pepper

Process garlic cloves in a food processor until they're finely chopped. Add the rest of the ingredients, including the reserved liquid, processing until until you have a smooth and creamy mixture.

Lemon Garlic Salad Dressing

This is a bright and fresh tasting dressing for your greens that is simple to prepare. As always, use the best quality olive oil you can find.

This dressing also is delicious for any salad with seafood.

1/2 clove garlic, minced
1 teaspoon salt
1 tablespoon lemon juice
3 tablespoons olive oil
pepper

Mash the garlic and salt together in the bottom of your salad bowl. Whisk in the lemon juice, then the olive oil, and check

14

the seasoning, adding pepper to taste.

You can make the dressing ahead of time, then just before serving, whisk the dressing to blend thoroughly, then toss the salad ingredients.

Mediterranean Salad Dressing

A tasty addition to your quality salad greens. If I'm making this for my husband, I do add the sugar. If it's just for me, I skip it. Experiment to tailor this to your own taste.

1/2 cup olive oil
juice of 1 lemon
1 finely minced garlic clove
1/2 teaspoon Dijon mustard
small pinch of sugar
salt and pepper

Whisk all the ingredients together well. Let sit for 10 minutes to infuse the garlic flavor into it all. Pour over your salad ingredients and gently mix.

Melon, Prosciutto, and Figs

Prosciutto is a dry-cured Italian ham that is usually thinly sliced. It is a bit expensive, but you don't use a whole lot.

Balsamic vinegar is becoming more widely available as its reputation and use grow. It gets sweeter when it's reduced, as in this recipe.

1/2 cup balsamic vinegar
1/2 ripe cantaloupe, seeded and peeled
4 thin slices prosciutto
4 ounces crumbled mild goat cheese
1 tablespoon extra virgin olive oil

freshly ground pepper

Put the balsamic vinegar into a small pan and cook over high heat until the liquid is reduced to 2 tablespoons and has thickened, about 10 minutes. Remove from the heat and let cool.

Cut the melon into 24 pieces. Slice each fig into 4 pieces, lengthwise. Put a piece of fig on a piece of cantaloupe, then roll up in a prosciutto slice. Divide all evenly onto 4 plates. Crumble the goat cheese over, then drizzle each serving with the reduced vinegar and a little olive oil.

Nicoise Salad

You can find many variations of this salad, but this is one I think is at least close to best.

1 large head Boston-lettuce leaves, washed and dried
1 pound green beans, cooked and refreshed in an ice-water bath
1 1/2 tablespoons minced shallots
1/2 to 2/3 cup basic vinaigrette
Salt and freshly ground pepper
3 or 4 ripe red tomatoes, cut into wedges (or 10 to 12 cherry tomatoes, halved)
3 or 4 new potatoes, cooked, peeled, and sliced
2 - 3 ounce cans chunk tuna, preferably oil-packed
6 hard-boiled eggs, peeled and halved
1 freshly opened can of flat anchovy fillets
1/3 cup small black Niçoise-type olives
2 to 3 tablespoons capers
3 tablespoons chopped fresh parsley

Toss the green beans with a little vinaigrette, then toss the tomato wedges in a bit of the dressing.

Mound the potatoes in the center of your servicing dish, put a mound of beans at each end, put mounds of tomatoes and mounds of tuna around the beans.

Put the egg halves strategically around, and then an anchovy that's been curled up on top of each egg.

Sprinkle everything with more vinaigrette, then sprinkle on the capers, and garnish it all with the parsley.

Orange And Carrot Salad

This is so good you'll forget that it's healthy. Be sure to section the oranges over a bowl to collect all the juice.

2 large oranges, peeled, pith removed, sectioned with membranes removed, juice reserved
1 pound carrots, well scrubbed and grated
1 teaspoon ground cinnamon
3 tablespoons fresh lemon juice
1 teaspoon orange flower water
pinch salt
1 tablespoon chopped mint

Toss everything except mint together. Chill. Before serving, garnish with the mint.

Pesto

Pesto is best known as a sauce for pasta, but don't let that limit your use of it. It's an excellent sauce for chicken and fish, as well.

This is the traditional recipe for pesto with basil and pine nuts, but the ingredients can be changed up according to your tastes and what's available at the market. You can use walnuts instead of the pine nuts, spinach instead of the basil, more or less garlic, etc.

1/4 cup pine nuts
3 cloves garlic
1 teaspoon salt
4 ounces fresh basil leaves, about 3 packed cups
2/3 cup extra virgin olive oil
1 cup freshly grated Parmesan cheese.

Toast the pine nuts in a skillet over medium heat until lightly browned, 5 or 6 minutes.

Put the toasted nuts, garlic, and the salt into a food processor and process until everything is finely chopped. Add the basil and continue processing until the basil is also finely chopped.

Keep the processor running slowly and drizzle in the olive oil. Process until everything is smooth.

Add the Parmesan cheese, pulsing just until the cheese is mixed in.

Radish Salad

This is not only delicious - it's also a very pretty salad. Another candidate for serving in a lettuce cup.

8 good sized radishes, trimmed, thinly sliced
1 minced shallot
3 tablespoons olive oil
1 tablespoon white wine vinegar
salt and pepper

Combine all the ingredients, then refrigerate for an hour before serving.

Red Wine Vinaigrette

Whip this up quickly, and toss with well-chilled greens just before serving.

3 tablespoons red wine vinegar
1/2 cup olive oil
salt to taste

Quickly whisk the ingredients together to emulsify a bit. Pour over the salad ingredients and gently toss to combine well.

Roasted Beet Salad

Beet salads are very popular now. Roasting gives beets a sweeter, earthy flavor that can win over beet haters.

2 large beets, scrubbed well, greens removed
3 tablespoons extra virgin olive oil
1 tablespoon finely chopped shallot
1 clove minced garlic
1 tablespoon apple cider vinegar
1/4 teaspoon Dijon mustard
1 1/2 teaspoon finely chopped fresh mint
2 teaspoons honey
1/2 teaspoon lemon zest
salt and pepper to taste
1 cup shredded romaine lettuce
2 ounces feta cheese

Preheat the oven to 400 degrees F.

Wrap each beet in aluminum foil and bake about an hour, until tender. Cool. Peel the beets and cut into 1 inch cubes.

Make the dressing: combine olive oil, shallot, garlic, apple cider vinegar, mustard, mint, honey, lemon zest, and salt and pepper.

Add 2 tablespoons dressing to the beets. Add 1 tablespoon dressing to the shredded lettuce.

Arrange 1/4 cup lettuce, topped with about 1 cup of the beets, sprinkle with feta.

Makes 4 cups.

Roasted Red Pepper Tapenade

While traditionally tapenade is a condiment served with crackers or bread, for us non gluten folks, it's delicious with fresh vegetables, raw or cooked, or as a sauce for meat, chicken, or fish.

You can use bottled red peppers or roast your own: roast whole peppers in a 500 degree F. oven for 30 minutes or so, until the skin is wrinkled and charred. Pop the peppers into a paper bag for a few minutes, letting the peppers cool a bit. Now you can just rub away the loosened skin, cut off the stem, and scrape out the seeds.

2 roasted red peppers, finely diced
20 pitted Kalamata olives, finely diced
1 ripe tomato, seeded and finely diced
2 garlic cloves, finely minced (should be about 1 teaspoon)
1/4 teaspoon freshly ground black pepper
2 teaspoons extra virgin olive oil

Toss everything together in a bowl and mix well but gently. Let sit for 30 minutes or so, to blend the flavors.

Sausage Stuffed Dates

Considered the diamonds of dates, Medjool dates are the preferred ingredient here. They are large, very sweet, and chewy. If you can't find or can't afford them, use the best quality date that you can.

Quality Italian sausage shouldn't have any grain filler, but be sure to check the ingredients label.

1/2 Italian sausage link
12 dates
3 tablespoons roasted almonds, finely chopped
1/2 cup mild goat cheese
2 tablespoons fresh parsley, finely chopped

Cook the sausage link for 15 minutes or so over medium heat, until it's done. Let it cool, then slice the link in half lengthwise, then crosswise into 12 pieces.

Combine the almonds and goat cheese in a small bowl. Separate into 12 portions and set aside.

Partially slice the dates down the center to remove the pit, being careful not cut them completely in half.

Assemble: put 1 piece of sausage and 1 portion of the cheese mixture into each date, mounding the cheese, repeat for each date. Sprinkle the chopped parsley over all.

Makes 12 pieces.

Shrimp and Melon Salad

This is a bright tasty salad that surprises with the taste of melon and shrimp.

2 cups leaf lettuce, torn into bite sized pieces
1/3 cup cantaloupe, in 1/2 inch cubes
1 finely chopped scallion, including green parts
1/2 diced avocado
1/2 pound large cooked shrimp, about 14 pieces

2 tablespoons balsamic vinaigrette
1 tablespoon finely chopped basil

Divide lettuce between 2 places. Do the same with the cantaloupe, scallion, and avocado. Mound half of the shrimp on each piece, drizzle the vinaigrette over, and sprinkle on the chopped basil.

Serves 2.

Simple Balsamic Vinaigrette

This is a very simple and very tasty version of a wonderful vinaigrette you can use on any number of menu items. Salads come alive, and it brightens the taste of vegetables.

3 tablespoons balsamic vinegar
1 tablespoon Dijon mustard
1 garlic clove, minced
1/2 cup olive oil
Salt and freshly ground pepper

Mix the vinegar, Dijon, and garlic, mashing it all together. Slowly drizzle in the olive oil so it emulsifies and thickens a bit. Correct the seasoning.

Simple Tomato Chili Pepper Salad

Everything a salad should be: quick and easy to put together, lovely on the plate, and taste with a little zip.

1 1/2 pounds tomatoes, cut into wedges
4 tablespoons fresh lemon juice
1 green chili pepper, minced
3 tablespoons minced parsley
2 tablespoons olive oil
salt and pepper to taste

Combine lemon juice, chili pepper, parsley, olive oil, and salt and pepper. Pour over tomatoes and gently toss.

Tomato and Cucumber Salad

Lots of interesting taste here. It takes a bit of chopping, but then comes together nicely. The refrigeration brings the flavors together.

4 anchovy fillets, chopped
3 tomatoes cut in wedges
1 green bell pepper, seeded, membrane removed, and cut into pieces
1 cucumber, peeled and cut into chunks
1 red onion, thinly sliced
1 minced garlic clove
1 cup feta cheese, cubed
1/2 cup sliced black olives
1/2 cup finely chopped basil leaves
1/2 cup chopped parsley leaves
3 tablespoons olive oil
1 tablespoon wine vinegar
1 teaspoon chopped thyme leaves
pepper and salt

Toss all of the ingredients together. Refrigerate for an hour before serving.

Tuna and Tomato Salad

Served in lettuce cups or over chopped greens, this salad is as pretty as it is tasty.

1 - 6 ounce can tuna, well drained
1 large ripe tomato, cut into wedges
1/2 onion, thickly sliced

salt and pepper to taste
2 tablespoons olive oil
1 tablespoon red wine vinegar

Combine all the ingredients and gently mix.

Tuna Potato Salad

A very tasty, light, and refreshing salad perfect for summer.
The capers add a little excitement to the tastes.

8 ounces new potatoes
4 tablespoons balsamic vinaigrette dressing
10 cherry tomatoes, cut in half
10 Kalamata olives, pitted and halved
1 tablespoon minced red onion
1 tablespoons capers
1 - 6 ounce can good quality canned tuna in spring water
4 cups mixed lettuce greens

Cover the potatoes in water and cook until they're fork
tender. Drain and cool.

Slice the cooled potatoes into 1/4 inch slices. Gently toss 1
tablespoon of the balsamic vinaigrette with the potatoes.

In a separate bowl, combine the rest of the ingredients,
except the greens. Add 2 tablespoons of the vinaigrette and
toss gently. Toss the greens with the remaining tablespoon of
vinaigrette.

To serve, put 1 cup dressed greens on each plate. Tope with
1/4 of the potatoes, then 1/4 of the tuna mixture.

4 servings.

Tuna Tartare

Be sure to use only sushi quality tuna. It can be expensive, but this is a marvelous treat. Serve it in lettuce cups for a nice presentation.

2 pounds very fresh sushi quality tuna, cut into 1/4 inch dice
1 1/2 tablespoons Dijon mustard
3 tablespoons sesame oil
salt and pepper
3 tablespoons finely chopped ginger
2 tablespoons finely chopped cilantro
1 avocado, peeled cut into 1/4 inch dice

Put everything in a large mixing bowl and mix it gently with your hands. Chill before serving.

Warm Leek Salad

Leeks might seem an unusual start for a salad, but they present nicely and taste great in this salad.

2 pounds leeks, well cleaned, white parts sliced lengthwise
1 tablespoon olive oil
salt and pepper to taste
2 tablespoons red wine vinegar
1 tablespoon water
2 minced garlic cloves
1 pound tomatoes, peeled and chopped
1/2 teaspoon dried thyme
pinch cayenne pepper
2 tablespoons chopped fresh basil

Heat the oil and saute the leeks for 5 minutes over medium heat. Add the salt and pepper, the vinegar, water, garlic, tomatoes, and thyme. Cover the pan and cook for 20 minutes, stirring occasionally, until the leeks are tender. Add cayenne and correct the seasoning.

Garnish with the chopped basil.

Warm Scallop Salad

This is an attractive dish, as well as being delicious. Be sure to watch the scallops carefully; overcooking them results in chewy little pellets in your salad!

2 pounds bay scallops
salt and pepper to taste
5 tablespoons olive oil, separated
2 cups sliced mushrooms
1 cup seeded tomatoes, finely chopped
1/4 cup chopped parsley
1/4 cup balsamic vinegar
2 bunches arugula, washed well, dried, large stems removed, chopped

Heat oven to 500 degrees F.

Arrange the scallops in a baking pan, season with salt and pepper, then drizzle 2 tablespoons olive oil over them. Bake for 7 or 8 minutes until the scallops are opaque and firm to the touch.

Heat the remaining 3 tablespoons of oil over medium-high heat. Toss in the mushrooms and cook them, shaking and stirring, until they become golden brown, 5 or 6 minutes. Add the tomatoes, parsley, and vinegar, along with the cooked scallops. Stir the mix carefully and cook just to heat through.

Arrange the scallops onto a bed of the chopped arugula, surround with the mushroom tomato mixture, and drizzle any remaining sauce over all.

II. Soup

2 Bean Soup

A hearty and filling soup, this must be started the night before you cook it so the beans can be soaked and picked through. The smoked ham hock adds a great depth of flavor. You can use any kind of dried bean you want, just be sure that they total 2 cups.

1 cup dry pinto beans or cranberry beans
1 cup dry white beans
1 tablespoon extra virgin olive oil
1 cup diced onion
1/2 cup diced celery
1/2 cup diced carrots
8 cups good quality low sodium chicken broth
1 tablespoon Italian seasoning
1/4 teaspoon freshly ground black pepper
1 smoked ham hock

Pick through the beans to remove any stones. Put into a pot where they will have room to double and add enough cold water to still cover them when they double. Soak the beans overnight, then pick through them to remove any that look bad. Drain the beans and rinse them.

Heat the olive oil over medium heat in your soup pot. Add the onion, celery, and carrots, and saute for 5 or 6 minutes, stirring. Add the beans and the rest of the ingredients to the pot and turn the heat to high. Bring to a boil, then lower the heat and simmer the soup for 2 1/2 or 3 hours, until the beans are tender. Remove the ham hock, shred the meat, and add it back into the pot.

Makes 6 cups.

Basic Bean Soup

This recipe is delicious with any sort of bean. While the traditional Mediterranean version would probably have white cannellini or cranberry beans, feel free to use your favorite, including navy beans, pea beans, chickpeas, or even big red kidney beans.

1 large coarsely chopped onion
3 medium carrots, well washed and coarsely chopped
2 garlic cloves, minced
2 tablespoons olive oil
2 cups dried beans, soaked overnight and drained
8 cups water or quality chicken stock
1 tablespoon fresh thyme
2 bay leaves
1/4 cup chopped parsley

Heat the oil over medium heat and add the onion, carrot, and garlic. Cook 15 minutes or so, until the vegetables are soft but not browned. Add the beans, the water, and the thyme and bay leaves. Cook the soup for 2 or 2 1/2 hours, adding more water as needed to keep the beans covered. When the beans are soft, check and adjust the seasoning.

You can puree some of the beans and add them back into the pot if you want a thicker soup, or you can thin too-thick soup with water, stock, or crushed tomatoes with their juice. You can also add a squeeze of fresh lemon juice to brighten the flavors and give the soup a touch of Greek.

Blender Gazpacho

1 1/2 pounds tomatoes, peeled and seeded
2 garlic cloves, minced
1/2 onion, chopped
1 carrot, coarsely chopped
1 cucumber, peeled and chopped

1 green pepper, seeded and chopped
2 parsley sprigs, chopped
4 tablespoons chopped fresh basil
juice of 1 lemon
3 cups tomato juice

Mix everything well. Process in batches in the blender. Check the seasonings and refrigerate.

Butternut Squash Soup

Butternut squash soup is a great comfort food on a cold day. This recipe has a great creaminess and bright flavor. Be sure to check the ingredients on your chicken broth if you don't make your own. For some reason, some manufacturers add wheat gluten.

2 medium butternut squash, about 3 pounds
1 tablespoon extra virgin olive oil
1 cup diced onion
1 teaspoon Italian seasoning
4 cups good quality low sodium chicken broth
1 garlic clove, finely minced
1/2 teaspoon salt
1/4 teaspoon freshly ground black pepper
1 tablespoon honey
1 1/2 teaspoons freshly grated ginger

Preheat the oven to 400 degrees F.

Cut squash in half and remove the seeds. Place the cut side down on a baking sheet and bake for 35 to 40 minutes, until a knife or fork can be easily inserted. Allow to cool, then remove the skin. Roughly chop the squash.

Heat the olive oil over medium heat, then cook the onions for 6 or 7 minutes. Stir in the Italian seasoning. Add the squash and the rest of the ingredients, and cook over low heat for 25

29

minutes.

Chilled Cucumber Soup

This is a wonderfully fresh and bright soup. It's a perfect start, especially for summers meals.

2 cucumbers, peeled and chopped
1 onion, chopped
5 cups good quality chicken broth
2 cups plain yogurt
2 scallions, chopped fine
salt and pepper
fresh dill, chopped

Put the cucumbers, onion, and chicken broth over high heat, bring to a boil, then lower heat and cook until the vegetables are tender, 10 minutes or so. Chill.

To serve, add the yogurt and scallions, then check the seasoning. Sprinkle with the dill to garnish.

Fish Stew

The fennel combined with seafood is a taste I like a lot. If you haven't used it before, don't be alarmed at how strongly it smells of licorice when you trim and slice it. It has more aroma than taste.

If you're not that familiar with cooking a fish soup, talk with your fishmonger about the kinds of fish and shellfish to use.

3 tablespoons extra virgin olive oil
4 cloves thinly sliced garlic
1 large thinly sliced onion
1 small fennel bulb, trimmed and thinly sliced
1 tablespoon orange juice concentrate

1 - 14 ounce can diced tomatoes
1/2 teaspoon red pepper flakes
1 cup dry white wine
5 cups bottle clam juice
2 pounds assorted shellfish (firm white fish and any
shellfish), cut into bite sized pieces

Heat the olive oil and add the garlic, onion, and fennel,
cooking for 10 minutes or so until the vegetables begin to
brown. Add the orange juice concentrate, tomatoes, red
pepper flakes, wine, and clam juice. Bring to a boil, reduce
the heat, and simmer for 30 minutes. Taste for seasoning.

Increase the heat to medium, and add the fish. Cook for 2
minutes, then add shellfish and cook 5 minutes or so, until
the shells open. Toss any clams or mussels that don't open, if
you're using them.

Fruit Soup

Summer in a bowl! Use any fresh fruits to vary the flavor.

1 pound blanched, peeled, seeded, and sliced peaches
1 pound pitted and sliced nectarines
2 pounds pitted and sliced plums
1 pound strawberries, hulled and cut in half
3 cups water
juice of 1 lemon
2 tablespoons clover honey
1 tablespoon tapioca
chopped fresh mint to garnish

Combine all the fruit with the water, lemon juice, and honey
in a saucepan over medium heat. Bring to a simmer, cover,
then let cook for 15 minutes. Stir in the tapioca, continuing to
stir until the soup thickens; remove from the heat. Serve the
soup either warm or chilled, garnishing with the chopped
mint.

Garlic Soup

Cooking the garlic slowly over low heat takes away the sharpness of the flavor. You'll be surprised at how good this soup is, especially if you make it with your own flavorful chicken broth.

6 whole heads of garlic, cloves separated and peeled
1/4 cup olive oil
1 tablespoon red chili flakes
6 cups good quality chicken stock
1/3 cup dry sherry
pinch of ground cumin
pinch of saffron
salt

Heat the olive oil over low heat and add the garlic. Cook, stirring occasionally, for 10 or 15 minutes, until the garlic is soft and cooked but not browned. Remove the cloves from the oil and crush into a paste, using a fork.

Stir the red chili flakes, the stock and the sherry into the pot. Bring to a simmer, then stir in the cumin and saffron. Add the garlic paste, mixing it in well, then check the seasoning. Cover the soup and simmer for 20 minutes.

Gazpacho

Bright and fresh tasting, here is summer in a bowl.

8 large tomatoes
1/2 cup diced celery
1/2 cup peeled, seeded, and diced cucumber
4 sliced scallions
1 clove garlic, minced
1 tablespoon fresh lemon juice
1 teaspoon lemon zest
1/2 teaspoon salt

1/8 teaspoon black pepper
1 tablespoon minced parsley

Cut an x into the bottom of each tomato. Blanch the tomatoes in boiling water for 30 seconds, then remove with a slotted spoon to put into iced water (easiest if done in two batches).

Peel the tomatoes, chop the pulp, and put into a food processor. Add the rest of the ingredients, and pulse a few times for a roughly chopped soup. Or process completely for a smoother soup, then strain to remove tomato seeds.

Chill thoroughly before serving. Garnish with finely diced cucumber, finely sliced green onion, or chopped fresh parsley.

Lentil Lemon Soup

The lemon and yogurt in this soup brighten up the flavor of the lentils. This recipe calls for vegetable broth, but made with a good quality low fat chicken broth, it presents a new flavor.

1 tablespoon extra virgin olive oil
1 cup diced onion
1/2 cup sliced celery, 1/4 inch slice
1/2 cup sliced carrots, 1/4 inch slice
8 cups good quality chicken or vegetable stock
2 cups red lentils
2 dried bay leaves
1 minced clove garlic
1 teaspoon dried oregano
1/4 teaspoon freshly ground pepper
1 tablespoon ground coriander
zest of one lemon
1 cup kale, shredded
1 1/4 cups plain yogurt, Greek preferred

chopped fresh parsley for garnish

Heat the olive oil over medium heat in a good sized soup pot. Add the onion, celery, and carrots, and cook for 5 or 6 minutes, stirring. Add the broth, lentils, bay leaves, garlic, oregano, pepper, coriander. Bring the soup to a boil, then reduce the heat and simmer for 30 minutes, occasionally stirring. Stir in the lemon zest and kale, and cook for another 5 minutes to wilt the kale.

Remove from the heat and remove the bay leaves.

Serve topped with a dollop of yogurt and sprinkle of parsley.

Makes 10 cups.

Lentil Stew

Delicious, filling, and healthy. Pass a bowl of grated Parmesan cheese along with the soup.

1 chopped onion
4 chopped cloves garlic
1 tablespoon olive oil
1 1/2 cups lentil beans, rinsed and drained
5 cups chicken broth
1 tablespoon Worcestershire sauce
1 - 15 ounce can diced tomatoes with their juice
1 bay leaf
1 teaspoon thyme
salt and pepper
2 potatoes, well scrubbed and chopped
4 chopped carrots
3/4 pound fresh spinach, well washed

Heat the oil, then add the onion and garlic, cooking until soft but not browned. Add the lentils, broth, Worcestershire sauce, diced tomatoes and their juice, the bay leaf, thyme, and salt and pepper. Bring to a boil, cover the pot, and lower the heat to a simmer, cooking for 30 minutes.

Add the potatoes and carrots, again bring to a boil, cover, and simmer for 25 minutes. Remove the cover, add the spinach, and cook another 5 minutes to wilt the spinach. Remove the bay leaf before serving.

Provencal Seafood Stew

This does take some time and work, but it is well worth the effort. An elegant and tasty dish for family or company.

2 tablespoons olive oil
3 chopped shallots
1 small leek, well rinsed, then chopped
1 tablespoon fennel seeds
2 cloves garlic, chopped
3/4 pound tomatoes, peeled and chopped
2 large pinches crumbled saffron threads
8 ounces white wine
juice and grated zest of 1 orange or large lemon
2 tablespoons chopped fresh dill
salt and pepper
4 cups good quality fish stock or clam juice
2 medium squid, cleaned and cut into thin rings
1 pound john dory, red bream, seas bass, hake, or cod fillets, cut into large cubes
12 clams, well cleaned
1/4 pound raw prawns in their shells
2 springs oregano, chopped

Heat the olive oil over medium heat and add the shallots, leek, and fennel seeds. Cook, stirring for about 5 minutes until the shallot is translucent. Add the garlic, stir for a minute, then add the tomatoes and saffron. Stir and cook until the tomatoes start to look cooked and wilted a bit. Add the wine, citrus zest, and the dill. Season, then cover and gently boil the mixture for 30 minutes.

Pull the pan off the heat. Carefully process the mixture in a food processor or blender, then press it through a fine sieve. Pour the strained mixture back into the pan, check the seasoning, and bring it back to a gentle boil, just above simmering.

Add the squid and cook for 15 minutes. Add the cubed fish, the clams, prawns, and oregano, cooking for 5 minutes more, or until the clams open. Discard any clam that doesn't open.

Let the soup sit for a couple of minutes for all the flavors to blend.

Tomato Basil Soup

The very best taste is with vine ripened tomatoes, but when they're not available, you can use the best quality canned ones. Look for a no salt added product. You then can add your own salt to taste.

1 tablespoons extra virgin olive oil
1 cup diced onion
2 ribs celery, chopped
1 tablespoon minced garlic
1 tablespoon dried basil
1 teaspoon sugar
2 - 14.5 ounce cans diced tomatoes
salt and pepper to taste

Heat the olive oil over medium heat, and add the onion, celery, and garlic. Stir and cook for 5 or 6 minutes. Add the rest of the ingredients, and bring the pot to a boil. Lower the heat to simmer, and cook for 25 minutes.

The soup can be served as is or it can be pureed in a blender in batches or by an immersion blender.

Makes 4 cups.

Tomato Lentil Soup

14 ounce can of crushed tomatoes
1 tablespoon olive oil
1/2 pound dried lentils, well rinsed in cold water
2 quarts water
1 chopped onion
2 chopped carrots
2 chopped celery stalks
4 stalks Swiss chard, well washed, trimmed, cut into 1 inch
strips
salt and pepper
grated fresh Parmesan cheese

Saute the tomatoes with the olive oil over medium heat for
about 15 minutes.

Bring the water to a boil in a large pot and add all the
ingredients except the cheese. Bring it all back to a boil, then
cover and simmer the soup for 40 minutes, stirring
occasionally, until the lentils are tender.

Pass the cheese separately.

Vegetable Soup With Quinoa

This is an easy soup to make, and it is delicious. Traditionally
made with orzo, we've substituted quinoa to maintain it as
gluten free.

This recipe is meant as a suggestion; feel free to use the
vegetables that appeal to you and are freshly available.
Cooked, sliced Italian sausage is a tasty addition.

1 tablespoon extra virgin olive oil
1/4 cup chopped celery
1/2 cup chopped onion
1/4 cup sliced carrots
1 - 14.5 ounce can low sodium diced tomatoes
4 cups low sodium chicken broth or vegetable broth
1 cup chopped zucchini
1 cup sliced mushrooms
1 clove finely minced garlic
1/2 cup quinoa
1 teaspoon Italian seasoning
salt and pepper to taste
chopped parsley for garnish

Heat olive oil over medium heat, add the celery, onion, and carrots, and cook for 6 or 7 minutes.

Add the tomatoes and their liquid, the broth, zucchini, mushrooms, garlic, quinoa, and Italian seasoning. Increase the heat and bring the soup to a slow boil. Cook for 25 minutes, and check the seasoning.

Serve garnished with a scatter of parsley.

Yield 5 cups.

White Bean Tomato Zucchini Soup

Lots of great layered flavors here in a hearty soup.

1/2 pound dried white beans, washed and picked over, soaked overnight
1 tablespoon olive oil
1 large chopped onion
4 minced garlic cloves
2 quarts water
bouquet garni: 1 bay leaf, 1 sprig parsley, and 1 sprig thyme tied together

1/2 pound new potatoes, scrubbed well and diced
1 pound tomatoes, peeled, seeded, and diced
1 tablespoon tomato paste
1/2 teaspoon dried thyme
salt and pepper to taste
1/2 pound zucchini, diced
4 tablespoons minced fresh basil
1 teaspoon fresh lemon juice
4 tablespoons freshly grated Parmesan cheese

Saute the onion and garlic, just until the onion is translucent.
Add the beans, water, bouquet garni, and diced potatoes.
Bring to a boil, reduce the heat, cover, and simmer for an
hour.

Add the tomatoes, tomato paste, thyme, and salt and pepper;
simmer another 30 minutes, until the beans are tender. Add
the zucchini, and simmer 10 minutes.

Remove the bouquet garni, then stir in the basil and juice.

Sprinkle with Parmesan or pass the cheese for each to add
their own.

Winter Squash Soup

Simple and delicious, this is a great start to dinner or a lunch
meal all by itself.

1/2 cup olive oil
1 white onion, chopped
1 pound winter squash, cut into 1 inch cubes
salt
4 tablespoons grated fresh Parmesan cheese
2 tablespoons minced parsley

Saute the onion in the olive oil until soft. Add the squash and
salt to taste, cover, and cook over medium heat for 10

minutes, stirring a couple of times. Add enough water to cover the squash, and cook it for another 30 minutes. Remove from the heat and sprinkle with the cheese and parsley.

III. Vegetables and Side Dishes

Asparagus with Lemon and Garlic

A lovely side dish, with a little bite of garlic and the brightness of the lemon.

2 tablespoons olive oil
2 pounds fresh asparagus, trimmed, woody ends snapped off
2 cloves minced garlic
salt and pepper
2 tablespoons lemon juice
1 teaspoon lemon zest
1 cup shredded Parmesan cheese

Heat olive oil over medium heat, add the asparagus, garlic, and salt and pepper. Cover the pan and cook, shaking the pan to move the asparagus around to lightly brown. Cook 7 minutes, until just crisp tender. Remove from heat, add the juice and zest, and gently mix well. Put onto serving plate, and sprinkle on the Parmesan.

Baked Onions

The quick saute caramelizes the sugars in the onions, bringing up the sweetness. They then bake until they're tender, absorbing the delicate flavor of the chicken broth. Just delicious!

6 tablespoons olive oil
3 pounds small white onions, trimmed and peeled
1/2 cup chicken stock
salt and pepper

Heat oven to 350 degrees F.

Heat the oil over medium high heat and saute the onions for

about 15 minutes until they're lightly browned on all sides. Transfer the onions to a baking dish just big enough to hold them in one layer. Add the oil from the pan, the chicken stock, and salt and pepper.

Bake about an hour, until the onions are tender, turning them occasionally, adding a little more stock if the pan starts to dry, but just enough to leave mostly oil left in the pan when all is done.

Baked Vegetable Omelet

Any fresh vegetables will do for this tasty and easy to make dish. The ingredients are merely a suggestion. Use what's available and tasty.

10 large eggs
1/4 cup thinly sliced asparagus
1/4 cup finely chopped red onion
1/2 cup oil packed sun dried tomatoes
1 cup fresh baby spinach
1/4 cup finely chopped bell pepper, any color
1 cup sliced mushrooms
3/4 cup ricotta cheese, drained
1/4 teaspoon salt
1/8 teaspoon freshly ground black pepper
1 tablespoon chopped fresh parsley

Preheat oven to 350 degrees F. Coat a 9 x 9 baking pan well with olive oil.

Beat the eggs well in a large bowl.

In a separate boil, toss the vegetables, cheese, and seasonings carefully until well mixed. Pour the beaten eggs over the vegetables and stir to combine.

Pour the mixture into the prepared pan. Bake until the eggs

are set in the center, about 40 minutes. Remove from the oven to a rack.

Run a knife around the sides, cut into 9 pieces, and sprinkle with the chopped parsley.

Basic Polenta

This dish is wonderful on its own, but even better as the beginning to lots of other dishes. Consider adding grated cheddar cheese or grated Parmesan cheese to the basic recipe. You can also use the polenta as a base for sauces or toppings of sauteed vegetables. Endless possibilities!

3 cups water
1 cup polenta
salt and pepper

Bring water to a boil. Slowly add the polenta and return to a boil, stirring constantly. Lower heat, and simmer, stirring frequently, for 20 to 25 minutes, until the polenta is thick and tastes done. Season.

Braised Fennel

Fennel is one of my favorite vegetables. It has definite anise aroma when you're cutting it fresh, then just a hint of that flavor when it's cooked.

2 bulbs fennel, trimmed and cut into quarters
3 tablespoons olive oil
2 cloves sliced garlic
salt and pepper
2 cups chicken or vegetable broth

Heat oil over medium heat, add the fennel, laying the flat side down on the pan. Add the garlic and seasonings, then cook, turning the fennel until it's beginning to brown. Add the broth, bring to a boil, cover the pot, and simmer for 30 to 40 minutes, the the fennel is tender and the liquid is mostly absorbed.

Broiled Eggplant With Garlic and Rosemary

The rosemary and garlic add wonderful flavor to the mild taste of the eggplant, but you shouldn't feel limited to only those. Be sure to keep the surface of the eggplant far enough away from the heat source to avoid burning the garlic and herbs.

2 pounds eggplant
salt
2 finely minced garlic cloves
1 teaspoon chopped fresh rosemary
pepper
2 tablespoons olive oil

Cut the eggplant in half lengthwise, then score the cut side, being careful not to cut to or through the skin. Sprinkle the cut side with salt and let it set for 30 minutes. Rinse it and pat dry.

Preheat the broiler, and arrange the racks so the eggplant will be no closer than 8 inches from the heat.

Sprinkle the cut side with the garlic, rosemary, and a bit of pepper, working the herbs into the cut parts of the eggplant. Brush with olive oil, and put the eggplant, cut side up, on the baking pan. Broil for 25 or 30 minutes until the eggplant is cooked through and tender. Baste with a little more oil halfway through the cooking.

Braised Zucchini with Lemon and Basil

The lemon perks up the taste of the zucchini. And what isn't better with fresh basil?

1 pound zucchini
salt
olive oil
1/2 teaspoon red pepper flakes
juice of 1 lemon
1 tablespoon slivered fresh basil leaves

Slice the zucchini into 1/4 thick pieces. Put into a colander and sprinkle salt over all. Allow to sit for 30 minutes or so, then rinse the salt off and dry the slices.

Preheat the broiler. Oil the bottom of a baking sheet, then arrange the zucchini slices over and brush the tops with more olive oil.

Put the pan about 10 inches below the broiler and grill the zucchini slices for 10 or 12 minutes until the tops are just beginning to brown.

Put the broiled slices on a serving dish and sprinkle with the pepper flakes and salt and pepper to taste. Chill.

Just before serving, sprinkle on the lemon juice and basil strips. Toss just to mix.

Broiled Zucchini

Broiling is a great way to emphasize the flavor of the zucchini. This is a quick and tasty preparation. I even got my husband to like zucchini for the first time.

2 pounds zucchini, cut into pieces 3/4 inches thick and 4 inches long

45

2 tablespoons olive oil
salt and pepper
2 tablespoons olive oil
2 minced garlic cloves
1 tablespoon white balsamic vinegar
1 tablespoon chopped parsley

Heat the broiler.

Toss the zucchini with 2 tablespoons olive oil. Put on a baking sheet, and sprinkle with salt and paper. Broil for about 4 minutes on each side. Mix the remaining oil, garlic, vinegar, and parsley. Pour over the zucchini and toss to coat evenly.

Chickpeas and Spinach

This dish improves with standing, so cooking it the day before you're going to serve it works very well. It can be served hot or at room temperature.

3/4 pound chickpeas, picked through and soaked in cold water overnight
4 tablespoons olive oil
2 onions, chopped
2 tablespoons ground cumin
5 chopped garlic cloves
juice of 1 lemon
1 pound fresh spinach, washed, drained, and chopped
salt and pepper

Drain and rinse the chickpeas. Put them in a large pot, cover them with water, bring to a boil, and cook for an hour. Strain the beans, but keep the liquid.

Add the oil to the saucepan, saute the onions for a few minutes, then add the cumin and the garlic. Cook for about 5 minutes, until it's aromatic. Add the chickpeas back to the pot and enough of the reserved liquid to cover them. Add the lemon juice.

Cover the pot and simmer another hour. Add the spinach, season, then mix well and cook another 20 minutes.

Garlic Basil Eggplant

What isn't good with garlic and fresh basil? Turn eggplant haters into eggplant lovers with this delicious recipe.

2 eggplants, washed, cut in half lengthwise
4 cloves minced garlic
3 tablespoons olive oil
2 teaspoons chopped basil
2 tablespoons Parmesan cheese

Preheat oven to 350 degrees F. Lightly oil a baking pan.

Cut a slice from the unpeeled side of the eggplant, just enough that it will sit cut side up in the baking pan.

Combine the garlic, oil, and basil, blending well. Spread 1/4 of the mixture over the up side of each eggplant piece. Bake for 45 minutes or until tender. Remove from oven and sprinkle with the cheese.

Garlic Broccoli

If you don't make your own chicken broth, be sure to check the label of any that you purchase. I've found some brands that add wheat gluten for some reason.

I got my husband to like - and actually request - broccoli by cooking it in chicken broth. The quick toss with the garlic is just icing on the cake.

12 spears broccoli
2 cups chicken broth
2 tablespoons olive oil
3 cloves minced garlic
2 tablespoons chopped parsley
salt and pepper

Cook the broccoli in the chicken broth in a covered pan until just crisp tender, about 7 minutes. Drain it well.

Heat the oil over medium high heat, then add the garlic and cook, stirring, just until the garlic starts to color. Add the broccoli, parsley, and salt and pepper to taste, stirring quickly just to combine.

Garlic Cannellini Beans

This is a quick and tasty dish that's filling, as well. It also offers up a good serving of protein.

2 - 15 ounce cans cannellini beans
5 cloves minced garlic
1 tablespoon olive oil
1/2 cup chicken broth
salt and pepper to taste

Rinse and drain the beans. Heat the oil, then saute the garlic just until it softens. Add the beans, chicken broth, and seasonings, then simmer 10 or 15 minutes, until most of the liquid is evaporated.

Garlic Roast Cauliflower

Another roasted vegetable and more garlic! For added plate appeal, sprinkle with some finely chopped parsley just before serving.

1 head of cauliflower, cut into 1 1/2 inch florets
2 tablespoons olive oil
2 cloves garlic, finely chopped or minced
salt and pepper

Preheat oven to 425 degrees F.

Combine cauliflower, garlic, and oil in a large zippered freezer bag. Toss well to coat the cauliflower, then arrange the florets in a single layer on a baking sheet. Roast until the cauliflower is tender and browned a bit, 25 or 30 minutes.

Garlic Sauteed Spinach With Mushrooms

This is a most delicious spinach preparation. Even folks who think they don't like spinach eat this at my house.

1 tablespoon extra virgin olive oil
4 cloves finely minced garlic
1/2 pound sliced mushrooms
salt and pepper
10 cups spinach leaves
1 ounce freshly grated Parmesan cheese

Heat the olive oil over medium heat, add the garlic mushrooms, and salt and pepper. Cook for about 5 minutes, tossing the mushrooms around the pan. Add the spinach and toss or stir to wilt, about a minute. Remove from the heat and add the Parmesan, tossing to distribute.

Garlic Spinach with Pine Nuts

Raisins and pine nuts add a nice flavor and texture surprise to this tasty spinach dish.

2 tablespoons olive oil
4 cloves chopped garlic

10 ounces well cleaned spinach
1 teaspoon fresh lemon juice
1/4 cup golden raisins, plumped with boiling water
4 tablespoons toasted pine nuts

Heat olive oil over medium high heat. Add the garlic and cook, stirring, until the garlic is just starting to turn color. Add the spinach and stir until it's wilted, 4 or 5 minutes. Mix in the raisins and top with toasted pine nuts.

Green Beans with Tomatoes

Pretty as well as tasty, the combination of the tomatoes and green beans, brightened with a bit of lemon, will bring raves from your diners.

1 cup finely chopped onion
1 clove finely chopped garlic
1/4 cup olive oil
3 pounds trimmed green beans, cut into 2 inch pieces, rinsed and drained, but not dried
2 cups chopped fresh tomatoes or drained canned tomatoes
1/2 teaspoon sugar
1 teaspoon salt
1 tablespoon lemon juice

Saute the onion and garlic in the oil over low heat until it is golden, about 15 minutes. Add the beans to the pot, stir well, then cover the pot and simmer for 5 minutes. Add the tomatoes, sugar, and salt, recover, and cook for 10 minutes. Add the lemon juice, and test the seasoning.

Grilled Asparagus With Lemon

I'm a sucker for fresh asparagus grilled this way. All the flavors are bright and fresh. This recipe is also good for grilling thick slices of zucchini or eggplant or mushrooms on a skewer.

Heat grill to medium, or heat broiler, arranging racks to be about 8 inches below the heat.

2 pounds fresh asparagus, woody ends snapped off
1/4 cup olive oil
salt and pepper
juice of 1 lemon, freshly squeezed

Drizzle the asparagus with the olive oil, then season with the salt and pepper. Arrange on the grill, or put onto a baking sheet if broiling. Cook, turning, until the asparagus is just crisp tender. Put on your serving platter and drizzle with the lemon juice.

Lemon Pepper Kale

Be sure to cut away the tough centers of the kale. You'll be surprised how flavorful this dish is.

1/2 pound kale, rinsed and trimmed well, sliced into 1/2 inch strips
2 tablespoons extra virgin olive oil
1 tablespoon finely minced shallot
4 finely sliced cloves garlic
1/4 teaspoon crushed red pepper flakes
1 tablespoon fresh lemon juice
salt and pepper to taste

Heat the oil over medium heat, then add the shallot, garlic, and red pepper flakes. Stir and cook for 2 minutes. Add the kale and cook another 3 minutes, stirring or shaking the pan constantly. Remove from the heat, add the lemon juice and salt and pepper to taste. Toss to mix.

Makes 2 cups.

Mushrooms In Wine

These ingredients all work well together, without masking the flavor of the mushrooms.

You can experiment with different varieties of mushrooms; all the ones I've tried were delicious in this recipe. Just be sure to clean the mushrooms carefully; grit isn't good.

1 tablespoon olive oil
2 minced shallots
5 minced garlic cloves
2 pounds mushrooms, cleaned, trimmed, and halved
1 cup dry white wine
1/2 teaspoon dried thyme
1/2 teaspoon dried rosemary
salt and pepper to taste
1/2 cup chopped parsley

Heat the oil over medium heat, and add the shallots and half the garlic. Saute until the shallots are tender, stirring often.

Add the mushrooms and the rest of garlic, then saute until the mushrooms start releasing their moisture.

Add the wine, herbs, and salt and pepper, then continue cooking for 20 minutes, until the mushrooms are tender.

Add the parsley, then check the seasonings. Serve warm.

Oven Braised Leeks

For a long time, the only way I used leeks was in potato leek soup. Then I found this delicious way to prepare them. Now they're a star side dish for just about anything.

8 leeks, white parts only, cut in half lengthwise and washed thoroughly

2 cups chicken stock
1/4 cup olive oil
2 tablespoons lemon juice
1/2 teaspoon dried oregano
1 bay leaf
salt and pepper

Heat oven to 375 degrees F. Arrange the leeks in a single layer in a baking pan.

Combine the remaining ingredients in a saucepan, and bring to a boil. Lower the heat and simmer for 10 minutes. Pour over the leeks, cover the baking pan with foil, and bake for 20 minutes, until the leeks are soft.

Remove the foil and continue to cook, letting the leeks start to brown and the cooking liquid to thicken.

Polenta With Sun Dried Tomatoes

The polenta is delicious served like mashed potatoes from the pot, or you can put it into an oiled 9 x 12 inch baking pan, refrigerated for later, then the portions are reheated by sauteing in a bit of oil for 4 minutes per side or so.

4 cups water
1 teaspoon salt
1 cup cornmeal
1 - 15 ounce can of corn, drained
1/3 cup oil pack sun dried tomatoes, chopped
1/2 cup freshly grated Parmesan cheese

Bring the water to boil and whisk in the cornmeal and salt. Reduce the heat to low, continuing to whisk to be sure cornmeal is evenly distributed and not lumped. Continue whisking or stirring for another 20 minutes or so. As the cornmeal cooks, it will start to pull away from the sides of the pan.

Add the corn and tomatoes, and continue cooking for another 5 or 6 minutes to heat through. Remove from the heat, and stir in the Parmesan cheese to blend.

Serves 6.

Quinoa Pilaf

Quinoa is an ancient Andean grain, recently rediscovered, especially good for folks looking to avoid gluten. It has tremendous health benefits. It's a little like rice or bulgur, with a little fluff to it.

1 cup water
1/2 cup quinoa
1 tablespoon extra virgin olive oil
1 minced garlic clove
1/3 cup chopped bell pepper
1/4 cup chopped scallions
1 cup diced tomatoes, peeled and seeded, but with juice
salt and pepper to taste
4 tablespoons crumbled feta cheese
4 tablespoons chopped parsley

Bring the water to a boil, add the quinoa, return to a boil, lower the temperature to low, cover the pot, and cook for 20 minutes.

Heat the oil over medium heat, then add the garlic and bell pepper. Cook for a few minutes, until the garlic is fragrant, then add the scallions, tomatoes, cooked quinoa, and salt and pepper to taste. Cook for a minute or two, just until all is heated through. Top each serving with the feta and a sprinkle of parsley.

Makes 2 cups.

Rice Stuffed Baked Tomatoes

Baked tomatoes always seem elegant to me, and I love the taste. These make a very pretty presentation and always bring raves from guests.

4 large firm tomatoes
6 generous tablespoons Arborio rice
4 garlic cloves, minced
salt and pepper to taste
12 fresh basil leaves, slivered
3 tablespoons chopped parsley
1/2 teaspoon dried oregano
4 tablespoons grated Parmesan cheese

Heat the oven to 375 degrees F. Oil a baking dish big enough to hold the tomatoes.

Cut the top off each tomato, about 1/4 of the way down, saving the top for the lid. Scoop out the seeds carefully, then scoop out the pulp. Chop the pulp, then mix with the rice, garlic, salt and pepper, parsley, oregano, and Parmesan cheese. Carefully fill the tomatoes, then put the tops back on. Put the tomatoes in the baking dish, cover with foil, and bake for one hour. Let stand a little to cool a bit before serving.

Risotto Milanese

This is the basic recipe for risotto. Once you have this mastered, which isn't at all difficult, you can consider adding other ingredients and flavorings.

7 cups chicken stock
4 tablespoons butter
1/2 cup finely chopped onion or shallot
2 cups plain white raw rice, preferably Italian (arborio) rice
1/2 cup dry white wine
1/4 teaspoon saffron threads, crushed to a powder

4 tablespoons soft butter
1/2 cup freshly grated Parmesan cheese

Bring the chicken stock to a simmer and leave on low heat.

Melt four tablespoons of butter over moderate heat, add the onions, and cook them for 5 or 6 minutes, until they're wilted but not browned.

Add the rice and stir it for 2 or 3 minutes to get all the grains coated in the butter. Add the wine and cook the rice until the liquid is almost completely absorbed. Add 2 cups of the heated stock to the rice and let it cook, stirring often, until almost all of the stock is absorbed. Add another two cups broth, stirring and cooking until the broth is again absorbed.

Stir the saffron into 2 cups of stock and let it steep for a few minutes. Then pour it over the rice. Cook until the stock is completely absorbed.

Test to see if the rice is tender. If it isn't, add the remaining stock 1/2 cup at a time until the rice is tender and creamy.

Carefully stir in the 4 tablespoons of butter and the cheese, mixing well, but taking care not to mash the rice. Serve it hot.

Roast Onions

You can use tiny onions, peeled kept whole, or mild sweet ones that are thinly sliced, such as Vidalia or Walla Walla sweets. Avoid big pungent onions.

1 tablespoon olive oil
1 cup onions
salt and pepper
1 tablespoon honey
1 tablespoon chopped fresh thyme

1 bay leaf
2 cinnamon sticks
1/2 teaspoon wine vinegar

Heat oven to 400 degrees F.

Heat oil over medium high heat, then add the onions. Stirring constantly, let the onions sear a bit. When they turn soft and brown and begin to caramelize, add the salt and pepper and honey. Mix well, and continue to cook for 3 minutes, stirring.

Remove the pan from the heat, add the thyme, bay leaf, and cinnamon.

Move the pan to the oven, and bake for 10 minutes. Remove from the oven, stir in the vinegar, and remove the bay leaf and cinnamon stick. Serve warm.

Rosemary Garlic Potatoes

Get away from boring potatoes as a side dish. These smell wonderful and taste delicious. They're baked with just a touch of oil, so nice and healthy as well.

2 tablespoons extra virgin olive oil
1 teaspoon fresh rosemary, finely minced
2 cloves garlic, finely minced
salt and pepper
1 pound well scrubbed red potatoes

Preheat the oven to 400 degrees F.

Combine the oil, rosemary, garlic, and salt and pepper. Quarter the potatoes and toss them in the oil mixture. Spread the potatoes on a baking sheets, and bake for 30 minutes, until they are brown and fork tender.

Sauteed Zucchini With Tomatoes

1 tablespoon olive oil
1 1/2 zucchini, sliced 1/4 inch thick
2 minced garlic cloves
1 pound chopped tomatoes
salt and pepper to taste
1 tablespoon chopped fresh basil

Saute the zucchini and garlic in the oil over medium heat for about 5 minutes. Add the tomatoes, season with the salt and pepper, and bring to a simmer. Simmer, stirring often, for 20 minutes. Stir in the basil and check the seasoning.

Sauteed Brussels Sprouts

You may think you don't like Brussels sprouts, but this recipe might just change your mind.

2 pounds Brussels sprouts, trimmed, washed, and cut in half.
salt
3 tablespoons olive oil
2 finely chopped garlic cloves
black pepper

Add Brussels sprouts to 2 quarts of boiling, salted water. Cook about 5 minutes or until just fork tender. Drain them well.

Heat oil over medium high heat, and add the garlic, cooking for 30 seconds, then add the Brussels sprouts, cooking and stirring for another 30 seconds.

Sauteed Spinach

You'll be surprised at how good spinach can taste when you add lots of garlic!

3 tablespoons olive oil
4 crushed garlic cloves
9 ounces spinach, well washed and left a little wet
salt

Saute the garlic in the oil until it's lightly browned. Add the spinach and salt, stirring to coat it well with the oil, and cover the pan. Cook for 4 or 5 minutes, just until the spinach is wilted.

Spicy Broccoli

Broccoli is one of nature's wonder foods, full of great nutrients and anti-oxidants. Your family will happily eats lots of it prepared this way.

2 pounds broccoli florets, separated
1 tablespoon olive oil
2 cloves garlic, minced
1/2 teaspoon red pepper flakes
1 tablespoon dry white wine
salt and pepper

Steam the broccoli for 8 minutes, until crisp tender, and drain it.

Saute the garlic and red pepper in the oil for 1 minute. Add the broccoli and wine, and cook, stirring for 3 minutes. Season with salt and pepper to taste.

White Beans with Tomato

Did you know white beans are a good source of protein? Just a 1/2 cup serving provides 7 grams of protein. Here is a tasty way to get that protein.

3 cups canned white beans, drained, liquid reserved
1 tablespoon olive oil
1 onion, chopped
2 minced garlic cloves
1 bay leaf
salt and pepper to taste
3/4 pound tomatoes, peeled, seeded, and chopped
1/4 teaspoon dried thyme
2 tablespoons fresh basil, chopped

Add enough water to the reserved liquid from the beans to make 1/2 cup.

Saute the onion and garlic in the oil until the onion is tender. Add the tomatoes and thyme, correct the seasoning, and simmer for 10 minutes. Add the beans, cooking liquid, and the basil to heat through. Check the seasoning.

Zucchini and Rice Casserole

1 tablespoon olive oil
1 minced onion
2 pounds zucchini, finely chopped
2 minced garlic cloves
2 eggs, beaten
2 ounces grated Gruyere cheese
2 tablespoons grated Parmesan cheese
1/2 cup chopped parsley
1/2 cup short grain brown rice, cooked
1/2 teaspoon dried thyme
salt and pepper to taste

Heat the oven to 375 degrees F. Oil a 1 1/2 quart casserole.

Heat the olive oil and cook the onion over low heat, stirring often until tender. Add the zucchini and garlic and saute for 10 minutes, stirring often.

Stir the cheeses into the beaten eggs, then the parsley, rice, thyme, and sauteed vegetables. Season to taste, and put all into the casserole. Bake 50 to 60 minutes, until the mixture is firm. Cut into squares and serve.

Zucchini Frittata

1 tablespoon olive oil
1 onion, chopped
2 cloves minced garlic
3 zucchini, well scrubbed and sliced 1/4 inch thick
salt and pepper
2 tablespoons fresh basil, minced
8 large eggs, beaten
1/2 cup grated Parmesan cheese

Heat oven to 425 degrees F.

Heat oil in an oven-proof skillet over medium heat, then add the onion and garlic, stirring until they're soft. Add the zucchini and salt and pepper, cooking and stirring for 6 or 7 minutes. Stir the basil into the eggs, then add the egg mixture to the skillet.

Put the skillet into the oven and bake the frittata for 20 minutes, until the eggs are set. Remove the skillet from the oven, turn the oven to broil, sprinkle the cheese on top of the eggs, and broil for 3 or 4 minutes, just until the cheese melts and browns a bit.

IV. Chicken

Baked Chicken with Tomatoes

Tasty, quick, and healthy. What could be better?

3 pounds chicken, cut into 14 pieces
14 ounce can crushed tomatoes
3 tablespoons grated Romano cheese
salt and pepper
2 tablespoons olive oil
1/2 cup white wine

Heat the oven to 400 degrees F.

Put the chicken in a single layer in a large baking dish. Cover with tomatoes, cheese, and salt and pepper. Drizzle the oil over, then the wine. Bake 40 minutes, until the chicken is cooked through and juices are clear. Turn the oven to broil and cook another 2 or 3 minutes to crisp up the skin.

Balsamic Vinegar Broiled Chicken

2 pounds boneless, skinless chicken breast
1/2 cup chicken stock
salt and pepper
1 tablespoon dry mustard
2 tablespoons sugar
4 chopped garlic cloves
1 cup white balsamic vinegar
2 tablespoons Dijon mustard

Put the chicken in a bowl or zippered freezer bag. Mix the rest of the ingredients, whisking to combine well. Pour the marinade over the chicken and refrigerate for 4 to 6 hours.

Heat the broiler. Arrange the chicken on a broiler pan or

baking sheet. Broil for 5 or 6 minutes per side, basting often with the marinade, until the chicken is done through and juices run clear.

Chicken Breast Packets

Delicious and easy to do. The chicken is cooked in foil packets with sauteed vegetables, steaming and allowing all the flavors to combine.

4 boneless skinless chicken breast halves, pounded to 1/4 inch thickness
salt and pepper
olive oil for brushing chicken
1 tablespoon olive oil
1 minced shallot
2 minced garlic cloves
1/2 pound mushrooms, sliced
1/2 teaspoon chopped fresh rosemary
1/4 teaspoon thyme
3 tomatoes, peeled, seeded, and chopped
zest of 1 lemon

Heat oven to 375 degrees F.

Cut 4 large pieces of heavy foil, large enough to fold over and generously cover a chicken breast. Brush with oil and put a chicken breast on half the sheet.

Saute the shallot and garlic in the oil until the shallot is tender. Add the mushrooms and stir, cooking 10 minutes. Add the herbs and tomatoes, and continue cooking and stirring for 8 to 10 minutes. Remove from the heat, stir in the lemon zest and salt and pepper to taste.

Spoon 1/4 of the sauce over each chicken breast. Fold the foil over the chicken and vegetables, then crimp the edges to seal the packet. Bake for 20 minutes. Be careful when opening the packets, as the escaping steam can burn.

Chicken Piccata

A very tasty way to prepare chicken. Fresh spinach leaves make a wonderful bed on your serving platter under the chicken. The lemon slices add to presentation, as does the sprinkling of capers.

4 - 4 ounce boneless skinless chicken breasts
salt and pepper
1 tablespoon extra virgin olive oil
2 tablespoons dry white wine or chicken broth
1 tablespoon fresh lemon juice
1/2 cup good quality chicken broth
3 tablespoons capers
thinly cut lemon slices, optional
1 tablespoon finely chopped parsley

Pound the chicken breasts until about 1/2 inch thick (put them in a freezer bag for less mess while you pound). Season the cutlets with salt and pepper just before adding them to the pan.

Heat the olive oil over medium heat, and add the chicken breasts, cooking 3 or 4 minutes per side until just cooked through, no longer pink in the middle. Remove the chicken from the pan and keep warm.

Deglaze the pan with the wine, stirring to get up the bits from the bottom of the pan. Add the lemon juice, chicken broth, capers, and lemon slices if using, and cook until the liquid is reduced by half and syrupy. Serve each breast with 1/4 of the sauce, capers, and lemon slices, and a sprinkle of parsley.

Chicken With 40 Cloves Of Garlic

Don't be afraid of all the garlic in this dish. Cooked this long and unpeeled, the result is a creamy light garlic taste that just flavors the chicken and pan juices. Pile the cooked unpeeled garlic in a bowl to be served separately; just squeeze the cooked garlic out of the skin.

3 tablespoons olive oil
1 - 3 to 3 1/2 pound chicken, cut into 6 pieces
40 unpeeled garlic cloves
2 sliced carrots
3 tablespoons chopped tarragon
4 sprigs thyme, chopped
2 tablespoons brandy
1/2 cup white wine
salt and pepper

Preheat oven to 325 degrees F.

Heat the oil in a large, heavy, oven proof pan or casserole. Add the chicken and cook for 8 to 10 minutes, turning, until it's golden brown. Remove the chicken from the pan, then add the garlic, carrots and herbs, and cook for another 4 minutes, stirring.

Put the chicken back into the pan, and pour the wine and brandy around. Cook for 4 minutes, sprinkle in the seasoning, cover the pan and put it into the oven.

Bake for 1 1/2 hours. Serve the chicken with the garlic cloves on the side to be squeezed the get the garlic.

Chicken With Tomatoes And Capers

The combination of the tomatoes, capers, and olives is dynamite with the chicken. This is another dish that's easy to put together, and then gives you time to finish cooking the rest of the meal while the chicken is baking.

1 pound boneless, skinless chicken breasts, pounded to 1/4 inch thickness
1 tablespoon olive oil
salt and pepper
1 - 8 ounce can of chopped tomatoes, drained
2 tablespoons capers, chopped
1/3 cup green olives, pitted and chopped
1/4 cup white wine
2 teaspoons fresh lemon juice

Heat the oven to 400 degrees F.

Lightly brush both sides of the chicken with olive oil. Put into a baking dish, season with salt and pepper, and top with tomatoes, capers, and olives. Drizzle the white wine over all. Bake uncovered for 15 to 20 minutes, until the chicken is cooked through and not pink.

Chicken with Tomatoes and Olives

3 to 4 pounds chicken, cut into 6 or 8 pieces
6 tablespoons olive oil
3 onion, coarsely chopped
2 chopped garlic cloves
1 tablespoons minced fresh thyme
1/2 cup finely chopped parsley
2 cups chopped tomatoes
1/2 cup dry white wine
1/2 cup sliced black olives
juice of 1/2 lemon
salt and pepper

Heat 3 tablespoons of the oil over medium heat. Add the chicken pieces, and brown on all sides. Remove the chicken from the pan.

Add more oil if needed, then add the onions and garlic, stirring and cooking until they're soft but not browned. Add the thyme, parsley, tomatoes and wine, stirring to get all the pan leavings into the sauce.

Add the chicken back to the pan, and cook stirring occasionally for 25 or 30 minutes, until the chicken is cooked through and the sauce has thickened. Add the olives and lemon juice, then correct the seasonings.

Garlic And Lime Broiled Chicken

A simple and delicious preparation for chicken, don't be concerned with the amount of garlic. Be sure to turn the chicken several times while broiling so the chicken is cooked evenly and thoroughly.

12 minced garlic cloves
salt and pepper
6 tablespoons lime juice
1 chicken cut into 8 or 10 pieces, skin on

Combine the garlic, salt and pepper, and the lime juice. Rub the chicken all over with the lime mixture. Cover and refrigerate for 2 hours.

Heat the broiler, then broil the chicken for about 30 minutes total, turning the chicken as it cooks. Cook until the chicken is cooked through, no pink inside, and the juices running clear.

Garlic Chicken In Wine

The alcohol cooks away, but if you don't want to use the wine and Cognac, you can use chicken broth. Serve this with steamed rice so you can get all the tasty sauce.

2 1/2 pounds chicken, cut in 8 pieces, skin removed
1 tablespoon olive oil
8 finely minced shallots
24 unpeeled garlic cloves
1/4 cup Cognac
2 cups dry rose wine
2 rosemary sprigs
2 thyme springs
salt and pepper to taste
chopped fresh parsley

Heat the olive oil over medium heat, add the shallots and garlic, and cook and stir until the shallots begin to lightly brown. Add the chicken pieces and cook for 5 minutes, stirring. Add the Cognac and cook until it evaporates. Add the wine, rosemary, thyme, and salt and pepper. Bring to a simmer; lower the heat to just keep to a simmer, and cook for 25 or 30 minutes, turning the chicken occasionally.

Remove the chicken to a platter, raise the heat on the pan, and reduce the liquid to 1/2 cup. Remove the garlic cloves, and pass the softened cloves separately to be squeezed alongside the chicken. Pour the sauce over the chicken and garnish with the chopped parsley.

Lemon Broiled Chicken

The combination of lemon, oregano, and chicken is common in Mediterranean cooking, with good and tasty reason. Turn and baste the chicken often for even cooking, and be sure the chicken is completely done, not pink, before serving.

1 bay leaf
1 cup chicken broth
2 tablespoons chopped fresh oregano
1/4 cup olive oil
1/2 cup freshly squeezed lemon juice
salt and pepper

2 pounds boned chicken breast, skin left on

Combine all the ingredients except the chicken and mix well. Put the chicken into a bowl or zippered freezer bag, cover with marinade, and refrigerate for 1 or 2 hours, moving the chicken around a few times to get marinade all through.

Heat broiler. Lay chicken skin side down on broiler pan or baking sheet. Broil for 6 or 7 minutes per side, basting often with the marinade.

Orange and Lime Broiled Chicken

Chicken just seems to be made for citrus. This simple recipe always brings lots of compliments. Garnish the plate with thin slices of orange and lemon.

2 pounds chicken breasts, skin on
3 crushed garlic cloves
juice of 1 orange
juice of 1 lime
salt and pepper

Put all the ingredients in a bowl or zipper freezer bag. Refrigerate for 30 minutes, turning a couple of times so marinade is well distributed.

Heat the broiler. Arrange the chicken, skin side down, on a broiler or baking pan and broil for 3 or 4 minutes. Turn the chicken over, brush with some of the marinade and broil for another 4 minutes. Repeat another two or three times, until chicken is done through and juices run clear.

Rosemary Chicken Breasts

Another combination of chicken, rosemary, and lemon. This tasty version may seem a little complex, with putting the herbs under the skin, but you'll find it easier than it sounds at first. Then simply bake the breasts until they're done through and the juices run clear.

4 chicken breasts, ribs and skin attached
salt and pepper
2 tablespoons olive oil
1 generous tablespoon minced rosemary
4 minced garlic cloves
1 tablespoon lemon zest

Preheat oven to 400 degrees F.

Mix the olive oil, rosemary, garlic, and lemon zest together.

Carefully slip your fingers between the skin and meat of the chicken breasts, careful to leave the skin attached at the sides. Spread 1/4 of the rosemary mixture under the skin of each breast.

Lay the breasts in a baking pan that holds them all in one layer, skin side up. Season the breasts with salt and pepper, then bake for 40 or 45 minutes, until the juices run clear and chicken is fully cooked.

V. Fish and Shellfish

Baked Fish with Olives and Capers

This recipe is great with just about any fish you have, and any cut of that fish. You can cook whole fish, steaks, or fillets this way, just adjust the cooking time for the thickness of the fish.

2 pounds fish
1 cup chopped tomatoes
1 teaspoon lemon juice
1 tablespoon capers
1/4 cup green olives, pitted and chopped
salt and pepper

Heat the oven to 400 degrees F. Lightly oil a baking pan big enough to hold the fish in one layer. Place the fish in the pan.

Combine the rest of the ingredients, check the seasoning, then pour the sauce over the fish. Put in the oven and cook for 25 or 30 minutes, until the fish is cooked, and the sauce is bubbling.

Baked Fish with Tomato and Cilantro

The cilantro and cumin in this recipe add a nicely different flavor. Serve this over steamed rice so you catch all the flavors of the sauce.

2 pounds firm fleshed fish, cut into serving sized pieces
2 tablespoons olive oil
1 medium onion, thinly sliced
2 chopped garlic cloves
1 pound tomatoes, seeded and chopped
1 tablespoon ground cumin
1 cup minced cilantro

71

salt and pepper

Heat oven to 350 degrees F. Lightly oil a baking pan big enough to hold the fish in a single layer. Add the fish.

Heat the oil over medium heat, and add the onion and garlic, cooking and stirring until they're soft but not brown. Add the tomatoes, cumin, and cilantro, and cook until the flavors blend well, about 10 minutes. Adjust the seasoning, then pour the tomato sauce over the fish. Bake for 20 minutes, until the fish is thoroughly cooked. Serve with the sauce.

Baked Red Snapper With Tomato

As well as being tasty, this is a very pretty dish to serve. The tomato adds a brightness to the flavor and the presentation, and the spinach adds a nice contrast. It has the added benefit of being quick and easy to prepare.

2 pounds red snapper fillets, rinsed and patted dry
salt and pepper
juice of 1 lemon
1 tablespoon olive oil
3 onions, chopped
2 minced garlic cloves
2 pounds tomatoes, chopped
1/2 pound fresh spinach, coarsely chopped
1 teaspoon paprika
1 teaspoon ground cumin
1 tablespoon tomato paste, dissolved in 1/4 cup water
1/2 cup dry white wine
1 bunch parsley, chopped

Heat oven to 375 degrees F. Oil the bottom of a baking dish, and lay the fish into it. Sprinkle with salt, pepper, and lemon juice.

Saute the onions and garlic in the olive oil, just until the onion begins to brown. Add the tomatoes, spinach, paprika, cumin, tomato paste water mixture, and the wine. Cook for 15 minutes, and check the seasonings. Pour the sauce over the fish, and bake for 25 or 30 minutes, until the fish flakes easily. Sprinkle with the parsley before serving.

Baked Shrimp with Tomatoes

2 tablespoons olive oil
1 medium onion, thinly sliced
1/2 cup dry white wine
1 1/2 pounds tomatoes, blanched, skinned, and chopped
1 teaspoon dried oregano
salt and pepper to taste
1 pound peeled and deveined shrimp
2 tablespoons chopped parsley

Heat the oven to 350 degrees F.

Heat the oil over medium heat and saute the onion until it's translucent, stirring. Add the wine and bring to a gentle boil. Boil for 4 minutes. Add the tomatoes, oregano, and check the seasoning. Mix well and simmer for 20 minutes, stirring occasionally, until the sauce is thick.

Mix in the shrimp and parsley, then put everything into a baking pan and put it in the oven. Bake for 20 minutes.

Baked Sole with Capers and Shrimp

If you haven't discovered how good capers are, this is an excellent place to start.

1 pound sole fillets
pinch of dried oregano
pinch of dried basil
salt and pepper

10 cherry tomatoes, cut in half
2 teaspoons capers
1/2 cup cooked salad shrimp
4 tablespoons grated Parmesan cheese
1 lemon, cut into wedges

Heat oven to 400 degrees F.

Lightly oil a baking pan big enough to hold the fillets in a single layer. Lay the fish in the pan, then sprinkle with the herbs and the salt and pepper. Scatter the tomato halves, capers, and shrimp around the fish. Bake for about 10 minutes, until the fish flakes easily.

Sprinkle the cheese over the top of the fish, turn the oven to broil, and then broil for 2 or 3 minutes until the cheese has melted.

Serve garnished with the lemon wedges.

Baked Tilapia

This is a simple and delicious way to cook fish, and it's good with any number of type of fish.

1 pound tilapia, cut into 4 fillets
1 tablespoon olive oil
3 cloves minced garlic
2 scallions, white and green parts minced
1/2 cup chopped parsley
salt and pepper
1 quartered lemon

Place fillets in a baking dish. Separately combine the oil, garlic, scallion, parsley, and salt and pepper. Pour over the fish, cover the dish, and put into refrigerator to marinate for 30 minutes.

Heat oven to 350 degrees F.

Uncover pan, and put it into the oven. Bake for 15 minutes or until the tilapia flakes easily.

Broiled Halibut With Dijon Vinaigrette

Halibut and Dijon are a great taste combination. The halibut holds up well to broiling, and the tomato Parmesan topping adds a great fresh flavor.

4 - 6 or 8 ounce halibut steaks
1/4 cup olive oil
1 tablespoon Dijon mustard
1 tablespoon white wine vinegar
1 large ripe tomato, peeled, seeded, and chopped
2 tablespoons freshly grated Parmesan cheese

Heat broiler. Arrange racks so the halibut will be about 4 inches away from the heat. Grease the pan with a little olive oil. Lay the halibut steaks into the pan.

Mix the mustard and vinegar in a bowl, then whisk in the oil. Brush the fish with the dressing, then put under the broiler for about 8 minutes, turning once halfway through. Remove the pan from the broiler.

Mix the tomato into the remaining vinaigrette, and spread it over the fish. Sprinkle the cheese over the tomatoes. Return the pan to the broiler and cook another minute or so until the topping is warmed and crisp.

Chive and Basil Prawns

The prawns here are lightly accented by the addition of sweet basil and mild chives. Delicious!

8 ounces large prawns, shelled and deveined
2 tablespoons olive oil
2 garlic cloves, thinly sliced
1/4 pound mushrooms, sliced
salt and pepper
2 tablespoons finely chopped chives
3 sprigs fresh basil, thinly sliced

Heat the oil over medium heat, and add the prawns. Saute, stirring for 3 minutes. Turn up the heat and add the mushrooms. Cook for another 3 or 4 minutes, until the prawns are cooked through, stirring constantly. Season to taste, then add the chives and basil, cooking and stirring for another minute or so until the the herbs look just wilted.

Citrus Roasted Fish

A firm fleshed white fish such as swordfish, halibut, cod, and hake is excellent for this dish.

1 pound fish, cut about 1 inch thick and into 4 pieces
2 tablespoons olive oil
2 minced garlic cloves
1 minced small onion
1/4 cup chopped parsley
2 oranges, zest removed then juiced
salt and pepper

Heat oven to 400 degrees.

Heat the oil over medium heat, add the fish pieces, and brown them quickly on each side, 1 or 2 minutes. Remove from the pan and put in a single layer in a baking pan.

Lower the heat to medium and add the garlic, onion, and parsley. Stir and cook until the vegetables are soft but not brown. Stir in the orange juice and zest, bring to a boil, and check the seasoning. Pour the sauce over the fish.

Bake for 20 minutes or so, until fish is just cooked through.

Serve with the pan juices.

Grilled Sardines With Lemon

If the only sardines you've ever tasted came from a can, you're in for a pleasant surprise. If you can't find fresh ones from your market, smelt will work, too.

1 1/2 pounds fresh sardines or smelt, cleaned
1 tablespoon olive oil
2 finely chopped garlic cloves
juice of 2 lemons
12 fresh mint leaves, sliced thinly

Rinse the fish in cold water and pat dry. Sprinkle with salt and pepper and toss with the olive oil. Let sit for 15 minutes, tossing a couple of times.

Grill the fish 3 inches from the heat, 2 minutes per side, until the flesh flakes easily. Allow to cool a bit, then carefully remove the skin. Sprinkle with the minced garlic and the juice from 1 lemon. Let marinate for an hour, then sprinkle with the juice of the other lemon and the sliced mint. Serve at room temperature.

Halibut and Potatoes

Simple and tasty, the key here is to move the pan around to keep the potatoes from sticking.

1 onion, thinly sliced
salt and pepper
2 potatoes, thinly sliced
3 tablespoons olive oil

2 pounds halibut, cut into steaks 1 inch thick
1/2 cup white wine

Heat the oil over low heat. Add the onion, sprinkle with salt and pepper, then put the sliced potatoes on top. Cover the pan, and saute for about 7 minutes until the potatoes are tender. Don't stir or uncover the pan, instead shake the pan a bit and move it in a circular motion over the burner. You'll be able to feel that everything's moving around and not sticking.

Season the fish with salt and pepper, then place the steaks on top of the potatoes. Pour the wine around it. Cover the pan again and bring the wine to a boil. Reduce the heat and let the fish simmer for 10 or 11 minutes, again moving the pan around to keep everything from sticking. The fish is done when it flakes and is opaque in the middle.

Halibut with Ginger and Saffron

This is an excellent recipe to use with any firm fish. While it calls for a small amount of cream to thicken the sauce, you can eliminate it and just reduce the pan juices.

4 halibut steaks, about 1 3/4 pounds total
1 - 1 inch piece of ginger, peeled and grated
2 large pinches of saffron
3 tablespoons olive oil
1/2 cup good quality fish stock or white wine
salt and pepper
3 tablespoons cream
2 tablespoons chopped fresh parsley

Heat the oil over medium heat in a pan large enough to hold the fish pieces in a single layer. Add the ginger and saute for a few minutes, stirring. Add the fish to the pan and saute for 5 minutes, turning a few times.

Add the stock or wine and the seasoning. Bring it to a gentle boil and add the crushed saffron threads. Simmer for another 5 or 6 minutes, until the fish is just flaking and opaque in the center. Remove the fish from the pan and keep warm.

Boil the sauce in the pan to reduce it. Add the cream and chopped parsley and simmer gently for a couple of minutes to marry the flavors and let the sauce thicken. Pour the sauce over the fish and serve.

Mussels Marinara

Serve these mussels in a soup dish so you can also serve lots of this delicious broth.

1 tablespoon olive oil
6 minced garlic cloves
1 cup chopped onions
28 ounce can crushed tomatoes
2 tablespoons lemon juice
1/2 cup white wine
2 tablespoons chopped parsley
1 tablespoon chopped fresh basil
3 pounds mussels, well scrubbed, beards removed

Heat the oil, and saute the garlic and onion just until the onions are translucent. Add the tomatoes with their juice, the lemon juice, wine, parsley, and basil; cover and cook for 4 minutes. Add the mussels, and cook 8 to 10 minutes, stirring occasionally to be sure the mussels open, discarding any that don't.

Mussels with Garlic and Wine

Mussels seem to have been created to be cooked in garlic and wine. The parsley garnish adds a nice green flavor as well as a lovely look.

2 tablespoons olive oil
6 garlic cloves, sliced
3 pounds mussels, well scrubbed and beards removed
1/2 cup white wine
1/2 teaspoon oregano
3 tablespoons chopped parsley

Heat the oil and saute the garlic for 30 seconds. Add the mussels, wine, and oregano. Cover the pan, checking occasionally that the mussels are opening, and stir a bit to move them around so they all can open. Cook for 8 to 10 minutes. Discard any that don't open.

Sprinkle the parsley over all, and serve the mussels in their broth.

Pan Seared Scallops With Orange Over Greens

Scallops turn into bullets when overcooked, so you'll want to watch them carefully and only cook 2 or 3 minutes per side. In this recipe, they combine with orange and avocado for an elegant and delicious meal.

3 medium oranges
2 tablespoons white balsamic vinegar
1 clove finely minced garlic
1 teaspoon Dijon mustard
1/4 teaspoon salt
1/2 cup extra virgin olive oil
12 large scallops
1/2 teaspoon fresh oregano
4 cups packed mixed salad greens
1 avocado, peeled and diced

Remove the zest from an orange to measure 1/4 teaspoon. Segment the orange: cut off the bottom so the orange can stand flat. Cut down the outside of the orange from top to bottom to remove the peel and the white pith. Holding the orange over a bowl to catch the juices, remove the segments by cutting along the inside of the membrane between the sections. Preserve the sections and juice.

Juice the other 2 oranges to make 1/2 cup of juice.

Make the salad dressing by combining the zest, vinegar, minced garlic, Dijon, and 1/4 cup of juice. Whisk in the 1/2 cup oil slowly until everything is combined.

Heat 2 tablespoons oil over medium heat. Add the scallops in two batches so you don't overcrowd the pan. Cook for 2 or 3 minutes without moving the scallops so they get a little browned. Turn and cook another 2 or 3 minutes, just until the scallops are cooked through. Set aside and keep warm.

To the skillet add 1/4 cup orange juice. Cook to reduce by half and so it looks like a glaze, 1 or 2 minutes. Remove the glaze from the heat, and mix in the oregano.

Toss the greens, orange sections, and avocado gently with the dressing. Divide the salad between 4 plates. Top each plate with 3 scallops.

Serves 4.

Poached Scallops

Scallop deliciousness here. Watch the scallops carefully; it's easy to turn them into rubbery pellets.

1 cup freshly squeezed orange juice
2 teaspoons finely grated orange zest
1 pound sea scallops
1 tomato, chopped
1 teaspoon chopped fresh marjoram
2 tablespoons low fat sour cream

salt and pepper

Bring orange juice to a boil over medium heat, add the scallops, then reduce the heat and cover the pan. Simmer 5 minutes, just until the scallops are opaque and tender. Remove the scallops from the pan and keep warm.

Add the tomatoes and marjoram to the pan and simmer for 2 or three minutes, until the sauce is reduced by half. Stir in the sour cream, let sauce thicken a bit, then season. Add the scallops back to the pan just to heat through.

Scallops With Mushrooms

The scallops are sliced horizontally, so you end up with thin coins of scallop that need only the briefest of cooking. The mushroom herb mixture is a lovely complement to the scallops.

10 sea scallops
2 tablespoons olive oil
2 garlic cloves, crushed
1 sweet red pepper, seeded and cut into cubes
2 tablespoons chopped parsley
1 tablespoon chopped chervil
salt and pepper

Slice the scallops horizontally into thin discs.

Heat the oil and add the mushrooms and pepper, stirring and cooking for 5 to 6 minutes. Season and add the garlic and herbs; cook for another 3 minutes.

Brush a separate pan with olive oil, heat over high, and sear the scallops a minute per side to brown them. Toss the scallops with the mushroom mixture and serve.

Seafood with Fennel and Orange

Ouzo is a Greek liquor made from grapes and anise, the anise flavor of the liquor and the fennel adding a nice complement to seafood.

1/4 cup olive oil
1 red onion, thinly sliced
1 finely chopped clove garlic
1 large fennel bulb, trimmed and thinly sliced
1 cup chopped tomato
1/2 cup orange juice
grated zest of 1 orange
1/3 cup ouzo
2 pounds firm white fish, cut into serving sized pieces
1/2 pound scallops
1 pound medium shrimp, peeled and deveined
salt and pepper
finely chopped parsley for garnish

Heat olive oil over medium heat, and add the onion and garlic. Cook, stirring, for 5 or 6 minutes, until the vegetables soften but aren't browned. Add the sliced fennel, cover the pan, and cook 10 minutes or so, until the fennel is softened.

Stir in the tomatoes, orange juice and zest, and the ouzo. Cook for another 10 minutes, until the sauce has thickened.

Add the fish and the scallops, cook for about 7 minutes, then add the shrimp, making sure it's submerged in the sauce, then cook another 5 minutes. Check that the seafood is cooked through, adjust the seasoning, and serve all with the sauce.

Shrimp and Scallops In Citrus

This is very good served over spinach that has been wilted with a little oil and garlic. It's also excellent over steamed rice.

4 ounces fresh orange juice
juice from 1/2 pink grapefruit
juice from 1 lime
juice from 1 lemon
1/2 teaspoon shredded orange zest
1/2 teaspoon shredded lime zest
2 tablespoons olive oil
1/2 pound large sea scallops, cut in half horizontally
12 large shrimp, peeled and deveined
salt and pepper
2 scallions, thinly sliced

Combine juices and zest in a bowl.

Heat the 2 tablespoons olive oil over medium high heat, then
add shrimp and scallops. Move and turn the seafood just
until it's done. Remove from the pan and keep warm.

Deglaze the pan with the mixed juices and zest, stirring to get
all the bits from the bottom of the pan. Cook until the liquid
is reduced by half and a little syrupy. Season.

Remove the pan from the heat, and add the seafood. Toss to
coat the seafood with the sauce.

Shrimp in Marinara

The marinara is cooked for only 10 minutes, so you can
identify all the tastes, and each beautifully complements the
shrimp.

1/4 cup olive oil
7 sliced garlic cloves
2 pounds jumbo shrimp, peeled and deveined
1 - 28 ounce can of crushed or diced tomatoes
1 teaspoon red pepper flakes

salt and pepper
3 tablespoons chopped parsley
12 large fresh basil leaves, chopped

Heat the oil and saute the garlic until it just starts turning golden. Add the shrimp, without crowding the pan, and cook for 1 minute on each side, cooking in batches if necessary.

Remove the shrimp and add the tomatoes, red pepper, and salt and pepper to the pan.

Bring the sauce to a boil, then reduce the heat and simmer the sauce for 10 minutes, stirring occasionally.

Add the shrimp, parsley, and basil to the sauce, raise the heat, and cook it for another 45 seconds to 1 minute, just to heat through.

Shrimp with Tomatoes and Feta

The feta adds a creamy kick to this dish. Be sure you don't saute the shrimp for more than 1 minute. They finish cooking in the sauce in the oven.

2 tablespoons olive oil
1 pound tomatoes, peeled, seeded, and chopped
2 minced cloves garlic
1 green pepper, seeded, membrane removed, and chopped
1 cup chopped parsley
1/2 teaspoon red pepper flakes
1 pound 16 - 20 sized shrimp, peeled and deveined
salt and pepper
1 cup crumbled feta cheese

Heat oven to 400 degrees F.

Heat olive oil over medium heat.

Saute the tomatoes, garlic, pepper, parsley, and red pepper flakes, stirring for 10 minutes.

Add the shrimp and cook 1 minute.

Adjust the seasoning.

Transfer the mixture to an ovenproof dish, sprinkle the feta over, and bake for 8 minutes.

Soy Baked Halibut

Be sure to use a wheat-free soy sauce (hint: read the label well). Tamari soy sauce is one to look for.

2 pounds halibut, cut into 4 pieces
4 teaspoons finely chopped ginger
2 teaspoons minced garlic
1/2 cup sweet Marsala wine
4 tablespoons soy sauce
pepper
1 tablespoon sesame oil

Preheat oven to 400 degrees F. Put the halibut in a baking pan.

Mix the ginger, garlic, wine, soy sauce, pepper, and sesame oil. Pour it over the halibut, then cover the dish with foil and bake 12 or 13 minutes.

Steamed Clams

If you're used to your steamed clams being only cooked in water or broth, the addition here of garlic and wine will provide a nice new taste.

2 tablespoons olive oil

2 thinly sliced garlic cloves
1 1/2 dozen littleneck clams, scrubbed
1/4 cup white wine
2 tablespoons chopped parsley
lemon wedges for garnish

Cook the garlic in the oil over medium high heat, about 30 seconds. Add the clams and white wine, raise the heat to high, and cook 3 or 4 minutes, stirring, just until the clams open, discarding any that don't. Sprinkle with the parsley and serve with the lemon wedges.

Swordfish with Capers

Any firm white fish will take well to this recipe. The lemon and capers add a new dimension to the fish.

6 tablespoons olive oil
6 - 6 ounce swordfish steaks, cut 1 inch thick
salt and pepper
3 tablespoons capers, chopped
4 tablespoons chopped parsley
juice of 2 lemons

Heat the oil over medium heat.

Season the swordfish steaks with salt and pepper, and cook the swordfish in the oil for about 4 minutes per side, cooking in batches if needed to keep the pan uncrowded. Remove the fish to a platter and keep warm.

Add the capers and parsley to the pan, then deglaze with the lemon juice, cooking briefly.

Pour the sauce over the fish and serve.

Tilapia with Tomatoes and Capers

This is a very tasty way to cook any fish. Use what's available fresh at the market.

1 pound tilapia filet
1 tablespoon olive oil
salt and pepper
1 - 8 ounce can of chopped tomatoes, drained
2 tablespoons capers, chopped
1/3 cup green olives, pitted and chopped
1/4 cup white wine
2 teaspoons fresh lemon juice

Heat the oven to 400 degrees F.

Lightly brush both sides of the fish with olive oil. Put into a baking dish, season with salt and pepper, and top with tomatoes, capers, and olives. Drizzle the white wine over all.

Bake uncovered for 15 to 20 minutes, until the fish flakes easily with a fork.

Tuna with Cannellini Beans

A delicious salad that's healthy and full of protein. Serve it on top of mixed greens, and it's pretty as well.

2 - 6 ounce cans tuna
1/2 red onion, thinly sliced
1 - 15.5 ounce can cannellini beans, rinsed and drained
salt and pepper
2 tablespoons white wine vinegar
2 tablespoons olive oil

Drain tuna and put into a good sized bowl, breaking it up. Add the onion, cannellini beans, and salt and pepper, tossing gently to combine. Add the oil and vinegar and toss to mix well.

Tuna with Fennel

1 tablespoon olive oil
2 garlic cloves, minced
4 fennel bulbs, thinly sliced
salt and pepper to taste
4 - 4 ounce tuna steaks
2 tablespoons chopped parsley

Saute the garlic in the oil for a few minutes until the garlic is
transparent. Add the fennel and salt and pepper. Cover and
sweat the fennel over low heat for 15 minutes, stirring
occasionally, until the fennel is tender.

Salt and pepper the tuna steaks. Cook them briefly in a
nonstick pan for 45 seconds on each side.

Put the tuna onto the fennel mixture, cover the pan, and
cook over medium heat another minute or so per side,
cooking just until the tuna is pink in the middle and soft to
the touch.

Sprinkle with parsley and garnish with lemon wedges.

Tuna With Tomato Caper Sauce

This is just simply delicious. Plenty of garlic, the sweet
acidity of the tomatoes, and the little bite of flavor that
capers add all make for a dish your friends and family are
sure to love. If tuna isn't to your liking, or it's too expensive,
use any firm fish you enjoy.

1 tablespoon olive oil
1/2 onion, finely chopped
8 chopped garlic cloves

1/2 cup capers, rinsed and chopped
2 1/2 pounds tomatoes, chopped

4 - 6 ounce tuna steaks
olive oil for grilling

Add the onion to the oil and saute, stirring, until translucent, then add the garlic and capers. Saute for 5 more minutes, then add the tomatoes. Cook, stirring often, for 20 minutes.

Brush the tuna with oil and grill or broil the fish for 8 minutes per 1/2 inch thickness, turning halfway through the cooking. Be sure not to overcook the tuna, it should still be pink in the middle.

Serve topped with the sauce.

Wine Braised Tuna

The wine adds a nice undernote to the tuna.

1 thinly sliced onion
1 minced garlic clove
1 sweet pepper, cut into strips
1 tablespoon olive oil
1 pound fresh tuna, cut into 1 1/2 inch thick steaks
salt
1 cup dry white wine
1 tablespoon capers, coarsely chopped
1 tablespoon shredded lemon zest

Heat the oil over medium low heat, and saute the vegetables for 15 minutes or until they're soft.

Remove them from the pan, turn the heat to medium high, then add the tuna, quickly searing both sides. Add the vegetables back into the pan, along with the wine, then bring to a boil. Lower heat and allow the fish to simmer for 10 minutes, or until fish is as done as you like.

Add the capers and lemon zest to heat through, then serve.

VI. Lamb, Pork, and Veal

Braised Lamb Shanks

This is a wonderful dish for early spring when you can get fresh lamb, although it does not suffer from using frozen. Use the best quality red wine you can afford.

If you buy canned broth, be sure to carefully read the label. Some commercial broths, unfortunately, contain wheat gluten.

4 - 4 ounce lamb shanks
1/4 cup extra virgin olive oil
2 stalks sliced celery
2 to 3 large sliced carrots
2 cups chopped onion
1/3 cup tomato paste
6 cloves finely minced garlic
1/2 teaspoon dried oregano
1/2 teaspoon dried rosemary
1/4 teaspoon pepper
2 cups dry red wine
4 cups good quality beef broth
2 bay leaves

Preheat the oven to 325 degrees F.

Heat the oil in a large oven proof pot over medium high heat and brown the shanks 3 or 4 minutes per side. Cook in batches so you don't overcrowd the pan.

Remove the shanks from the pan, lower the heat to medium, and add the celery, carrots, and onion. Cook until the onions and celery start to wilt.

Add the tomato paste, garlic, herbs, and pepper. Stir for a

few minutes to blend the flavors, then add the wine, broth, and bay leaves, mixing well and scraping up the bits on the bottom of the pan.

Add the shanks back to the pot and bring it all to a boil. Cover the pot and put in the oven. Bake for 2 hours, until the shanks are tender. Skim the fat from the surface before serving.

Serves 4.

Braised Veal Shank

Braising insures tenderness and deep flavor. If you can't find veal shanks, try this recipe with beef shanks. You may have to ask your butcher specifically for them or to have them ordered.

2 tablespoons olive oil
4 pieces of veal shank, about 2 pounds
5 fresh sage leaves
1/2 cup white wine
1 cup quality beef or chicken stock
5 pieces fresh or dried orange peel, pith removed
6 basil leaves, chopped
salt and pepper

Heat the oil over medium high heat in a pan big enough to hold the shanks in a single layer. Add the shanks and brown the meat quickly on both sides to a golden brown.

Add the sage leaves, then pour in the wine. Cook for a couple of minutes, then add the stock, orange, and salt and pepper.

Lower the heat and cover the skillet. Cook, simmering, turning a few times, for 1 1/2 hours, or until the meat is very tender. Sprinkle the basil over all, simmer for a few more minutes to incorporate the basil flavor, and then serve.

Garlic Lamb Chops

Garlic, rosemary, and lamb are just about a perfect combination. Add a subtle mustard topping after the chops are broiled and just wait for the compliments.

8 - 4 ounce lamb chops
4 cloves minced garlic
1/2 tablespoon rosemary
3 tablespoons Dijon mustard
juice from 1 lemon
2 tablespoons olive oil
salt and pepper

Turn on broiler and let heat. Place rack so the chops will be about 4 inches from the heat.

Mix garlic and rosemary together. Put lamb chops in a single layer on a broiler pan, then rub garlic and rosemary over their surface.

Broil chops to desired doneness, 3 or 4 minutes per side for medium rare.

Mix together the mustard, lemon juice, oil, and pepper. Serve with a spoonful of the mustard mixture spread over each chop.

Roast Leg of Lamb

Garlic and rosemary combine for a classic and traditional preparation for lamb. It makes an impressive presentation when carved at the table.

4 finely minced garlic cloves
salt and pepper

2 tablespoons chopped fresh rosemary
2 tablespoons olive oil
1/4 cup Dijon mustard
6 to 8 pound leg of lamb, bone in, trimmed of excess fat.

Heat the oven to 350 degrees F.

Combine the garlic, salt and pepper, rosemary, olive oil, and mustard, mixing well. Brush the mix all over the lamb, then roast the lamb for about 1 hour 15 minutes until the internal temperature is 130 degrees for medium-rare.

Let the leg rest for 20 minutes before carving.

Roast Pork Florentine

4 pounds trimmed pork loin
1 teaspoon dried rosemary
8 whole cloves garlic
1/4 cup water
1/2 cup quality red wine
salt and pepper

Preheat oven to 325 F.

Poke the surface of the pork with a sharp knife, just deep enough to hold the garlic cloves. Press the cloves with a little of the rosemary into the cuts in the pork.

Put the pork loin into a baking pan, add the water and wine, and sprinkle with salt and pepper. Bake, basting occasionally, for 2 to 2 1/2 hours, until pork is tender and still moist, to an internal temperature 145 F.

Allow to rest for 10 minutes before slicing. It will continue to cook to reach 150 or 155 degrees.

Roasted Pork Loin

Pork found in markets today is a much leaner meat than you may have believed, and it's been bred to be a healthier option.

The pork will continue cooking while it's resting, reaching about 150 degrees, which is the recommended temperature of roasted pork now. This may seem too low if you're used to cooking to 165 degrees or more, but it is sufficient for modern pork, and you might be surprised at the better flavor and moistness.

4 pounds boneless pork loin
2 tablespoons olive oil
coarse salt
1 tablespoon garlic powder
1 tablespoon dried thyme
1 tablespoon black pepper
1 tablespoon parsley flakes

Rub the pork loin all over with the oil. Separately combine the remaining ingredients, mixing well, then rub that over the pork. Refrigerate for at least one hour, or up to overnight.

Heat the oven to 350 degrees F.

Put the pork, fat side up, in a baking pan. Cook for 1 hour 15 minutes, until the internal temperature is 145 degrees. Remove from oven, tent with foil, and let sit for 20 minutes before slicing.

Veal Marsala

This is also very good with boneless, skinless chicken breasts, pounded thin. Cook the chicken for 3 or 4 minutes per side to cook through.

1 1/2 pounds veal cutlets, pounded thin
salt and pepper
3 tablespoons olive oil
3 cups cleaned, thinly sliced mushrooms
1/2 cup Marsala wine
1 cup chicken stock
2 tablespoons chopped parsley

Season the veal with salt and pepper, then saute it in oil over medium heat, about 2 minutes per side. Remove from the pan and keep warm.

Add the mushrooms to the pan, and cook for 3 or 4 minutes, until the mushrooms lose their moisture and begin to brown.

Add the Marsala and boil for 2 minutes, then add the chicken broth and boil until the mixture is reduced by half.

Return the veal and the accumulated juices to the pan, spooning the sauce and mushrooms over the meat. Sprinkle with the chopped parsley.

Veal Piccata

This is equally delicious with chicken breasts that are boned, skinned, and pounded thin. Cook the chicken 3 or 4 minutes per side.

1 pound veal cutlets, pounded thin
salt and pepper
2 tablespoons olive oil
1/2 cup chicken stock
1/4 cup lemon juice
1 tablespoon butter
1 tablespoon chopped parsley

Season veal with salt and pepper. Saute in the olive oil over medium high heat about 2 minutes per side. Remove from pan and keep warm.

Pour the oil out of the pan, and deglaze with the chicken stock and lemon juice. Boil for 1 minute, remove the pan from the heat, and swirl in the butter.

Pour the sauce over the veal, and sprinkle the chopped parsley over all.

Veal Scaloppine

This is a classic dish that never fails to please.
If you can't find veal, or prefer not to eat it, chicken makes a fine substitute. Use boneless, skinless breasts that have been pounded to a thickness of 1/8 inch. Saute for 4 minutes per side to be sure it's completely cooked through.

1/4 cup chicken broth
1/2 cup chopped onion
4 cloves minced garlic
1 12 ounce can diced tomatoes
4 tablespoons dry red wine
1/2 teaspoon dried oregano
1/2 teaspoon dried basil
1 tablespoon capers

1 pound boneless veal, trimmed of fat, pounded 1/8 inch thick
salt and pepper
2 tablespoons olive oil

For the sauce, combine broth, onion, garlic, tomatoes, wine, herbs, and capers in a saucepan. Bring to a boil, then lower the heat. Simmer the sauce for 20 minutes.

Heat the oil over medium high heat. Season the veal with salt and pepper, then saute quickly, 2 minutes per side. Serve covered in the sauce.

VII. Fruit and Desserts

Apple Compote

Another simple delicious dish to satisfy your sweet tooth, yet that will still please guests.

2 pounds apples, peeled, cored, and sliced
3 tablespoons lemon juice
2 tablespoons clover honey
1/4 cup unsweetened apple juice
1 cinnamon stick
1/2 teaspoon ground allspice
1/4 teaspoon freshly grated nutmeg
1/2 teaspoon vanilla

Heat oven to 350 degrees F. Lightly grease a 2 quart baking dish.

Toss the apples well with the lemon juice, then add the other ingredients, and mix well. Bake for 1 hour. Serve warm or chilled.

Fig and Apricot Compote

Compotes are sweet treat with the health benefits of fruit. You can, of course, use any fruit that is available and tasty. This one has a touch of lemon that intensifies the fruit taste. You can chop the fruit in a food processor, but be careful not to overload the machine. Pulse a few times to get the fruit chopped but not pureed.

8 ounces stemless dried figs, finely chopped
6 ounces dried apricots, finely chopped
3 ounces crystallized ginger, finely chopped
2 cinnamon sticks
1 cup sugar
2 cups water

juice of 1 lemon
1 teaspoon apple cider vinegar

Put all the ingredients into a pan, stirring to combine, over medium heat.

Bring it all to a boil, then lower the heat and simmer for 45 minutes, stirring occasionally, until most of the liquid has evaporated.

Makes 3 cups.

Lemon Minted Melon

Cantaloupe is such a great fresh flavor. Here with a touch of mint and lemon, it is refreshing, as well. It's just sweet enough to satisfy that dessert craving.

The trick to finding a good ripe melon is to note that it seems heavy for its size, and when you press the blossom end, it gives a bit and gives you the scent of cantaloupe.

1 medium ripe cantaloupe
1/3 cup sugar
1/4 cup water
1 tablespoon finely chopped fresh mint
1 teaspoon lemon zest

Halve the cantaloupe and remove the seeds. Peel and slice into 12 wedges.

Combine the sugar, water, mint, and lemon zest in a saucepan, and cook over medium heat to melt the sugar.

Allow the syrup to cool, then drizzle it over the cantaloupe wedges.

Madeira Poached Figs

Simplicity with extraordinary good taste.

1 1/2 cups Madeira
1 pound fresh figs, cut in half
1 tablespoon clover honey

Over medium heat, bring the Maderia to a simmer, and cook for 5 minutes.

Add the figs and simmer another 10 minutes (5 or 6 if the figs are very ripe).

Remove from the heat, and allow it all to cool.

The figs can be served warm or chilled.

Peach Compote

Extremely simple, extremely delicious, this dish will hush up that sweet tooth craving.

3 pounds sliced peaches, blanched, skin and pits removed
2 tablespoons fresh lemon juice
2 tablespoons clover honey
1/2 teaspoon ground cinnamon
1/2 teaspoon freshly grated nutmeg
1/2 teaspoon vanilla extract

Heat the oven to 350 degrees F. Lightly butter a 2 quart baking dish.

Toss the peaches with the other ingredients and pour into the baking dish.

Bake for 55 minutes.

Serve warm or chilled.

Pears Poached in Chianti

The Chianti and port wine give the pears a beautiful ruby color and, of course, great taste. The length of cooking time means the alcohol burns off.

1 bottle good quality Chianti
2 cups port wine
3 cinnamon sticks
juice and zest of 1/2 lemon
1 cup sugar
6 pears, peeled

Bring all the ingredients except the pears to a boil.

Add the pears and poach for 25 minutes. Remove the pears.

Discard the cinnamon sticks and lemon zest, then boil the liquid to reduce until it's thick, about 10 minutes.

Strain the liquid, and serve the pears with a drizzle of the sauce over.

Plum Compote

Compotes are an excellent dessert whether you're avoiding gluten or trying to lose a little weight. You can get creative with the fruit, using what looks the best and is freshest.

3 pounds ripe plums, halved and pitted
1/4 cup sugar
1 cup water
1 tablespoon Crème de Cassis liqueur (black current liquor)

Preheat oven to 350 degrees F. Arrange plums in a baking

pan, cut side up.

Combine the sugar and water in a saucepan, bring to a boil, and cook, stirring, for 5 minutes, until it becomes syrupy.

Pour the syrup over the plums, then drizzle the crème de cassis over all.

Bake for 45 minutes.

Poached Seasonal Fruit

This recipe works well for just about any firm fruit, such as the pears, peaches, and plums included here.

1 bottle good quality white wine
1 cup sugar
1 cinnamon stick
juice and zest from 1 lemon
1 fresh ginger slice, 1/2 inch thick
2 pears, peeled, cored, and halved
2 peaches, peeled, pitted, and halved
2 plums, peeled, pitted, and halved

Combine wine, sugar, cinnamon stick, lemon juice and zest, and the ginger over medium heat. Bring to a boil, cook until sugar is dissolved, about 5 minutes.

Reduce heat to a simmer, and add the fruit, gently stirring.

Cook for another 5 minutes, and remove from the heat. Let it all cool.

The fruit can be served now, drizzled with the poaching liquid. Or the fruit can be refrigerated after cooling until serving time.

Serves 4.

Vanilla Panna Cotta

Panna Cotta, or cooked cream, is a traditional Italian dessert. Here it's a simple vanilla, with a deeper flavor from a vanilla bean. Add some berries alongside or over it for a brighter flavor and look.

1/4 cup chilled reduced fat milk
2 1/2 teaspoons unflavored gelatin granules
1 1/2 cups reduced fat milk
1/4 cup sugar
1/4 cup heavy whipping cream
1/2 vanilla bean, cut lengthwise, seeds scraped

Sprinkle the gelatin granules over the 1/4 cup milk, stirring. Let the mixture rest for 10 minutes.

Combine the 1 1/2 cups milk, sugar, cream, and vanilla pod and seeds in a saucepan over low heat. Heat for 10 minutes or so, until the sugar dissolves and the mixture is near a simmer.

Add the gelatin-milk mixture and cook for another 2 or 3 minutes to be sure the gelatin is dissolved.

Remove from the heat, and discard the vanilla bean.

Pour the mixture evenly into 4 ramekins or dessert cups. Refrigerate 2 hours or overnight.

Serves 4.

Afterward

I hope you've enjoyed these recipes and found them helpful and delicious.

I would very much appreciate your review of this book at amazon.com. It takes only a minute and helps others know whether they should invest their money. And, of course, I hope you'll tell them to do just that!

About Chef Judi

Chef Judi graduated from Western Culinary Institute in Portland, Oregon, and then was recruited to a fine dining restaurant in Alaska. She returned to Oregon to open her own successful catering firm. She now spends her time cooking for friends and family, experimenting in cooking techniques, and developing recipes.